Setting Up for Infant/Toddler Care:

Guidelines for Centers and Family Child Care Homes

Revised Edition

**Annabelle Godwin and Lorraine Schrag,
Infant Task Force Co-Chairs
San Fernando Valley Child Care Consortium**

National Association for the Education of Young Children—Washington, D.C.

Photos copyright by
Robert Meier/Cover, 126
Marja Bergen/ix
Sharon Rosewoman/xii, 89
Marilyn Nolt/1, 8, 14
Francis Wardle/4, 68, 103
Renaud Thomas/10, 34, 44, 58, 78, 97, 104
April S. Haase/15
Cleo Freelance Photography/16, 22
Jeffrey High Image Productions/24, 62
Subjects & Predicates/26 top, 33, 36, 45, 64
Hildegard Adler/26 bottom, 27 top
Dave Halsey/27 bottom
Jean-Claude Lejeune/29, 86
Blair Seitz/35
Ellen Galinsky/48, 86

Gallery of Images—Burkey/49
Robert Koenig/53
Christina Tolomei/55
Rich Rosenkoetter/56
Ellen Levine Ebert/57
Diane Crafts/59
Robert Godwin/60, 87
Janice Mason/61
Faith Bowlus/63
Nancy P. Alexander/65, 73, 88
Cheryl A. Ertelt/80
Robert Hill/83
Jerry Baker/85
Shulamit M. Gehlfuss/95 (all)
Mary K. Gallagher/102

**National Association for the Education
  of Young Children**
1509 16th Street, NW
Washington, DC 20036-1426
202-232-8777 or 1-800-424-2460

The National Association for the Education of Young Children (NAEYC) attempts through its publications program to provide a forum for discussion of major issues and ideas in our field. We hope to provoke thought and promote professional growth. The views expressed or implied are not necessarily those of the Association. NAEYC wishes to thank the authors, who donated much time and effort to develop this book as a contribution to our profession.

Library of Congress Catalog Card Number: 96-68452

ISBN Catalog Number: 0-935989-75-7

NAEYC # 228

Editor (of revised edition): Carol Copple; *Design and production:* Jack Zibulsky and Angela S. Dixon; *Editorial assistance:* Penny Atkins, Sandi Collins, and Anika Trahan; *Illustrations (Appendix A):* Dilworth Design.

Printed in the United States of America.

Contents

Infant Task Force Roster

The following members of the Infant Task Force of the San Fernando Valley Child Care Consortium each have had 15 to 30 years of experience working with infants and young children.

Annabelle Godwin, M.A.

Professor Emeritus, Infant Studies and Child Development, Los Angeles Mission College, San Fernando

Lorraine Schrag, M.A.

Executive Director, Child Care Resource Center, North Hollywood; former Director, Child Care Centers for Infants and Preschool Children, Inglewood

Rose Bromwich, Ed.D.

Professor Emeritus, Department of Educational Psychology and Counseling; Director of the Program for Early Parent-Infant Education, California State University, Northridge

Alice Chu, M.P.H.

Health Educator, Los Angeles County Department of Health Services

Bobbie Edwards, M.A.

Program Director, Child Educational Center, Jet Propulsion Laboratory/Cal Tech, La Canada; Child Development Instructor, Glendale City College

Linda Gordon, B.A.

Director, Parents Infant Care Services, Santa Monica

Ellen Khokha, M.A.

Director, The Growing Place Child Care Center, Santa Monica

Harriet Kleinman, M.A.

Parent-Child and Infant Development Specialist/Consultant, San Fernando Valley

Phyllis Lauritzen, Ph.D.

Former Family Day Care Provider and Project Director, Child Development Associates Credential Program for Family Day Care, Long Beach City College; Faculty, California State University at Sacramento

Fran McHale

Family Child Care Consultant, Encino

Marjorie Morris, B.S.

Consultant, Child Care Challenges, Encino

Jackie E. Tishler, M.S.

Child Development and Family Child Care Consultant, Los Angeles

JoEllen Tullis, M.S.

Director, Head Start, Child Care Resource Center, North Hollywood

Ellena Weeks, B.A.

Former Child Care Coordinator, Kaiser Permanente, Southern California

Preface

Needs for quality group care of infants and toddlers are at an acute stage as the number of married mothers working outside the home increases, the divorce rate rises, the number of women becoming single mothers increases, and single parents return to the work force earlier in young children's lives. The Infant Task Force that created this set of guidelines for quality group care has provided a signal service to those who need the know-how to create supportive environments for the very young. The task force has provided examples of the kinds of equipment, personnel practices, room arrangements, uses of time and space, toy selection, and health and safety practices that every family child care provider or child care center director must consider once the decision to include infants and toddlers in a program has been made. On the practical economic level, the authors have provided clear examples of the costs of quality infant/toddler care. Detailed budgets help figure costs of creating groups of different sizes within the child care environment. The advice on keeping group size small and a ratio of no more than three infants to one caregiver is very sound.

In addition to practical dollars-and-cents information and explicit technical assistance for making purchasing decisions and setting up environments, there are guidelines for carrying out routine procedures fundamental to the care of infants and toddlers. Reasonable, clear suggestions for handling diapering and helping toddlers learn to use the toilet are given. The authors are particularly sensitive to issues of parent-staff relationships, which can be a critical factor in the adjustment of both baby *and*

family to out-of-home care. Fears and concerns of parents are noted. Ways to help parents deal with separation anxieties and feelings of guilt (often prevalent when tiny ones are left with someone other than their mother) are frankly, gently, and reassuringly discussed.

This book offers developmental guidelines that will assist the alert caregiver or director in knowing when an infant in group care is having developmental problems needing early remediation. Professionals, rather more than other people, are aware of and generally accept wide variability in infant functioning and in ages of achievement of developmental milestones. Specific suggestions for alerting staff when preventive or remedial measures *do* need to be undertaken are an especially welcome inclusion in this book.

The appendixes provide a potpourri of forms that directors and staff will want to study in order to select the recording forms and parent-staff communication forms most suited to their needs. Record keeping is very important when small children are in care. The authors have provided a rich selection of record forms from which to choose. The references that follow the chapters are also an excellent source of training materials and publications that directors and training specialists will want to consult for pre- and inservice staff training as they begin the thoughtful hard work needed to prepare for providing infant/toddler care.

Perhaps best of all is the philosophy that permeates these guidelines. This book recognizes that babies are very special people. They need bodily and emotional nurturance and affirmation on an intimate level that secures them a safe milieu in which to explore, rest, feed, love, and develop. Infant/toddler staff are very special. People who care for babies are not replaceable classroom cogs. They must be generous with body loving, responsive to cues of distress, able to take turns in infant/adult communication games that may be wordless but full of intimate meanings and contacts. Their knowledge of developmental theories, such as those of Piaget, Mahler, and Erikson, must be reflected in the sensitivity with which they select environmental experiences requiring tries and efforts toward more mature behaviors from the little ones in their care. They need to know research "ammunition" to help them respond to inappropriate parental demands that they teach babies to read, toilet train babies too early, or leave babies on their own when they require snuggling and carrying for emotional nourishment even once they are able to toddle.

These guidelines respect the infant caregiver as a very special person. Counsel for salary guidelines and costs for service reflect respect for the professional who will care for infants and toddlers. As pressures for infant/toddler care rise in society, so do pressures for custodial, warehousing care or for low-paid, untrained personnel. Babies are inarticulate and unable to be precise about ecological conditions and personal considerations that are essential for their optimal care and for their growth and learning. These guidelines can serve as a model for advocacy for babies. They clarify the directions, practices, and interactions most likely to facilitate the provision of optimal care for our very young. Along with the dollars-and-cents advice and the specific suggestions for materials and techniques, these guidelines support efforts to provide quality infant/toddler care environments. This compendium should be used frequently as a resource whose succinct but thorough collection of suggestions will be useful prior to and certainly during the adventure of and commitment to providing high-quality care for infants and toddlers.

—*Alice S. Honig, Ph.D.*
College for Human Development
Syracuse University
Syracuse, New York

Introduction

A Philosophy of
Infant/Toddler Care

Lorraine Schrag

With increasing numbers of infants in need of child care, the demand for infant care programs has grown. Technical assistance regarding program components and workable practices specifically geared to infant and toddler care, however, is not readily available.

To meet this need, the San Fernando Valley Child Care Consortium convened a task force made up of experienced providers from centers and family child care homes, as well as child development educators, to provide technical assistance to people starting or operating infant care programs. The main concerns of the task force were to identify characteristics unique to infants and toddlers and to promote standards of quality in child care programs.

Infants—indeed, children of all ages—must be given optimum opportunity for growth and development. Adults who care for infants must be educated and experienced in understanding children's needs and in setting up an environment responsive to these needs. They must recognize children's growth patterns so they can present materials and opportunities that encourage children to move to the next level of development. Understanding developmental levels and skills is especially critical for adults working with children who do not yet have language. It is essential to educate infant/toddler care providers about current findings and recommendations to maintain the constant link between child development knowledge and child care programs.

Because infant care is labor intensive, it is expensive to provide and costly for parents. Most child care centers that are able to offer infant care at reasonable fees to parents do so by spreading administrative and other costs over their preschool and other programs. Another solution to the high cost of infant care is family child care systems or satellite family child care homes attached to child care centers. To maintain quality, providers need to inform parents about the components of infant care that make it costly; these components cannot be compromised and so must be paid for.

The task force recommends a 1:3 ratio even though child care licensing in some states—California, for example—allows a 1:4 ratio of providers to children younger than age 2. There must be enough adults to guarantee the safety of active toddlers at all times. One adult to four children is a minimum standard, and consideration must be given to how one adult spends time with four infants. Diapering, for example, is a one-to-one activity, as is feeding. What happens to the other three infants while the adult is engaged in such one-to-one activities? The problem also exists if there are only *two* other infants but is a little easier to manage.

Likewise, consideration must be given to ratios during adult lunch breaks or attention to personal

Encourage parents to visit the child care setting whenever possible.

A Philosophy of Infant/Toddler Care

needs. It is important to have extra staff members available to work in the infant room when the regularly scheduled provider is out of the room. This way the mandated ratio can be met at all times. That such ratios should continue to be met even when children are sleeping is supported by the need to shift attention to other classroom requirements, such as disinfecting toys, changing crib linen, and washing surfaces.

Group size and provider-child ratios affect the quality of a program. We recommend that the maximum number of infants or toddlers in a group in a child care center not exceed 12; smaller group size is preferable. Even if square footage allows more children in a room, it is wise to limit the number to 12.

Infants and toddlers need a sense of orderliness. Too many adults and children in a room contribute to a sense of chaos and disorganization. Babies need intimacy and individual attention. In addition, a smaller group facilitates infection control by limiting each child's exposure to other children.

Whether infant care is provided in a center or a family child care home, a home-like atmosphere should be the model to offer an environment familiar and natural to the infant and to enhance a sense of warmth.

It is important to set up infant care programs that facilitate a team approach with parents. Parents often struggle with the decision to place their infant or toddler in care. To ease parents' transition into using an infant care program, providers must work closely with them, gathering information about the child's routines at home and maintaining communication verbally and/or by charting the child's day in the care setting.

Each child's chart should contain the type and quantity of foods and liquids the child had during the day and the times of feedings. Diaper changes, sleep times, and other significant events should be recorded. In addition, parents should be informed by phone about bruises, cuts, or other injuries so that they are not unduly alarmed when they arrive for pickup and see their child.

At pickup time, both provider and parent should review the chart information to obtain an understanding of the various components of the child's day. This helps create consistency for the child and builds cooperation between provider and parent. Provider and parent also should share general information about the child. Parents know more about their children than anyone; providers know more about children in groups. Pooling information enables both parents and providers to understand and share in the care of the child.

Encourage parents to visit the care setting whenever possible. By observing the children, parents can get a broader sense of children this age, as well as a more personal understanding of the individual children in their child's group. Parents will see how providers interact with, and model positive language and behaviors for, the children. It is often reassuring for parents to discover that other parents have similar experiences with their children and child care.

A sound philosophy of infant care is based on the interrelation of provider, parent, and program in ways that are supportive to parents, nurturing to children, and enriching to staff.

Considerations
in Infant and
Toddler Care

Chapter 1

What Are Parents Concerned About?

Harriet Kleinman

Child care professionals have learned that children are best served when providers have some understanding of the children's primary world at home. They also know that a spirit of partnership with parents promotes a higher quality of child care and that maintaining open lines of communication is an important means to that end.

We invited approximately 50 mothers who were considering or had recently begun using child care for their infants to discuss their concerns. The following is a summary of the feelings they expressed about child care issues.

The concern most frequently mentioned by the mothers was *lack of supervision*. This concern was buttressed, in many cases, by the mothers' observation of the care setting. For example, a mother bringing her 10-month-old to a center at 7:00 A.M. found only one staff person available for six or seven young children, a practice that is not even legal in most states. How many infants can a caregiver focus on at once? Even though additional help was expected shortly, this mother felt that one person was being stretched too thin for this important period of greeting and separating. She left the center feeling anxious.

Mothers also worried that other demands on providers would shift priorities from their children. One parent expressed her concern about the abrupt diversion of a family child care mother's attention to her own children when they come home from school. This parent felt her infant *might be neglected when "tender loving care" was needed* in the late afternoon hours. Other parents worried that providers might not really care if their children were uncomfortable or unhappy and in need of special attention at a busy time of day.

A parent worried that her quiet, "good" baby might be ignored in favor of loud complainers and that her child might not receive needed protection from more aggressive children. In a similar vein, the mother of an active, assertive toddler wanted reassurance that her child would be helped to "settle down" and learn to get along with his peers. In essence, these parents were saying that *they wanted their children to be seen as individuals* and to be cared for with regard to their special temperaments. They wanted their children's emotional and physical needs to take priority over concerns with schedules and order.

Health is another major concern of mothers. These mothers wondered whether their children would have more illnesses in a group setting. What would happen if their children became ill away from home? Would the provider tell them if their children were exposed to a child in the group who had a contagious disease? Several mothers said they would have to deal with their own guilt about their choices if their children were sick a great deal. And they wor-

Parents want their children to be seen as individuals and to be cared for with regard to their special temperaments. They want their children's emotional and physical needs to take priority over schedules and order.

Part I: Considerations in Infant and Toddler Care

ried about the logistics of special arrangements in case of illness: Would their jobs be jeopardized?

The mothers wanted more than custodial care for their children but did not seem highly concerned about "enriching experiences." Many mothers *wanted their infants and toddlers to be exposed to music, books, and interesting toys but were not looking for "reading readiness" activities.* The mothers we met (all in parent education programs) were aware of the importance of play, social interaction, and exploration, and they generally believed that their children would have opportunities for such activities in a child care setting, perhaps even more so than in their own homes. (Some parents do seek early academic programs and need guidance in understanding age-appropriate curricula; see "Providing Learning and Growth Experiences for Children," Chapter 4.)

Primarily, these parents were hoping that their children would feel loved, secure, and happy each morning when they went to child care. But paradoxically, several parents also expressed concern about their children becoming "too attached" to child care providers. Some mothers appeared torn between their desire that their infants or toddlers enjoy the nurturance of a loving "substitute mom" and their own need to feel "irreplaceable" to their children. They wondered if their children would be so angry about going to child care that they would reject them at the end of the day. And if their babies cried at pickup time, would other people think they were not good mothers?

In addition to these major concerns, parents mentioned worries about *costs, travel distances, conflicting approaches to discipline,* and *the need to monitor their infant/toddler's child care setting.* Alert to child sexual abuse issues, parents today are asking: "How do I get away from work to drop in?" "How do I really know what's happening when I'm not there?" "How do I stay vigilant and informed without antagonizing the child care provider whom I really like, truly need, and want to trust?" These are real issues that are not easily resolved. They are excellent topics to explore in staff meetings and parent discussions.

Providers should give parents good, clear messages from the start and indicate that expressions of parental concerns are welcome. This can be done through informal conversations, flyers, posters, questionnaires, phone calls, interviews, and group meetings—and especially through providers' reactions when parents *do* voice concerns. When problems are identified, providers should convey a nondefensive, problem-solving attitude. This approach will help parents feel that they are working *with* the providers as a team, with the mutual goal of optimal care for the children.

Parents often are understandably anxious and ambivalent about placing their infants and preverbal toddlers in group care settings. Without encouragement, however, they might not express their feelings to the child care providers. The providers' task of fostering constructive interchanges is not always an easy one, but making the effort is a worthwhile endeavor. Even taking the first step—letting parents know that their concerns are important—can be fruitful. Success in developing a partnership with parents will certainly reward providers with an opportunity for more optimal service to the children in their care.

Chapter 2

Helping the Child Adjust to the Setting

Phyllis Lauritzen

The infant's adjustment to a child care situation is a critical first step in development that forms the basis for future relationships with the outside world. Adjustment does not mean an absence of crying but an active involvement with the people and things in the child care environment.

Adjustment means learning to trust other people, learning to feel comfortable in a new setting, and learning even at a nonverbal level that "I am a separate person and I can cope with life on my own with the support of caring people." A quality infant program can fulfill a parent's need to work or go to school and an infant's need to grow and learn about the world beyond the home.

The adjustment process

The adjustment process for each child is unique and may involve different stages. At first the child may feel, "I have been left in a strange place with strange people. What is happening? Where is my mommy?" A preverbal infant who doesn't understand that Mother or Father will be back can be seriously distressed. An understanding adult who empathizes with a grieving child can provide the support necessary to help the infant gradually overcome and conquer fears and learn to trust and enjoy the new experience. The goal is not to deny grief or distress but to work through it.

There are individual differences in adjustment to new child care settings. Some infants and toddlers breeze through the transition with relative ease. Some seem to adjust well at first but then have a delayed reaction several weeks or a month later. Some seem to have difficulty from the beginning.

What is the cause of these variations in adjustment? It is the interaction of the attributes of the child, the feelings and attitudes of the parents, the characteristics of the caregiver, and the features of the child care environment.

Factors that influence adjustment

Attributes of the child

Being in less than ideal health definitely affects adjustment to and enjoyment of the child care setting. For infants identified as being at risk (such as preterm infants, those with diagnosed genetic or congenital disorders, and those with chronic illnesses), the adjustment period may be longer. These infants may require extra attention and careful monitoring by the caregiver and the parent. You may want to consult with the child's pediatrician. (See "Caring for Infants with Special Needs," Chapter 5.)

The age of an infant influences adjustment. Infants younger than 6 months generally adjust more rap-

Children have less time to miss their parents when there are interesting things to look at and manipulate.

idly. According to some research, infants between 6 and 15 months of age are in a period when separation anxiety is likely to occur, and therefore this age group may have more difficulty separating from the mother (or father). Other research has shown that toddlers between 15 months and 2 years of age may have even more difficulty, depending on the quality and type of their previous separation experiences.

Temperament is perhaps the most important attribute of the child that influences adjustment. Some children adjust easily and positively to new experiences; others need more time but can adjust with help and empathy from the important adults in their lives.

Attitudes and feelings of the parent

Research has shown that the quality of the relationship between the infant and the primary caregiver—most often the mother—influences future social relationships. Apparently, the infant's basic trust acquired through his or her first social interactions is an attitude that transfers to new situations.

Reasons for working, job satisfaction, and feelings about combining parenthood and working outside the home affect parent's acceptance of using child care, which is communicated to the infant through tone of voice, posture, gestures, and body tension or lack of tension.

The parent's trust of and feelings about the person caring for the child are conveyed both to the infant and to the caregiver and influence the child's adjustment. The parent is a very important link in facilitating the adjustment process.

Characteristics of the caregiver

There seems to be agreement among authorities in infant care that the most important factor affecting quality is the child care provider. A warm, knowledgeable, growing, caring person who appreciates and empathizes with very young children and who has the ability to interact positively with parents and co-workers has the qualities needed to become an outstanding infant caregiver.

Limiting the number of adults providing care to any infant or toddler to as few as possible supports the formation of relationships. In family child care, the adults who provide care are, by necessity, limited to the provider and perhaps an assistant. For center care, suggestions on the assignment of primary and secondary caregivers are given in the section "Prosocial Environment" in Chapter 9, "Setting Up the Environment." And for primary caregivers, see Chapter 16, "Family Child Care Systems and Satellite Homes."

Continuity of care with a limited number of caregivers in a stable environment allows positive feelings to develop between the infant and the caregiver. Through a continuous relationship, the caregiver develops a personal interest in and knowledge of the infant, thus enhancing the ability to engage in quality interactions. The infant gradually adjusts and builds trust in the new relationship.

Another key factor affecting continuity of care in all care situations is the stability of the staff and how long the caregiver stays in the position. The national turnover rate for center child care is 53% per year (National Center for Early Childhood Workforce 1992). The turnover rate in family child care is even higher.

Features of the child care setting

An adult-child ratio of 1 to 3 and a group size of 12 or fewer children give providers the time and energy to pay individual attention to each child as the need arises. For the child with an adjustment problem, this attention can mean the difference between total distress and learning to cope and trust a new situation.

The availability of developmentally appropriate play materials and the freedom to explore in a child-safe environment make the new setting exciting and interesting. Children have less time to miss their parents when there are interesting things to look at, manipulate, and act upon.

The presence of other infants and children in the environment provides a constant source of stimulation in the child care setting. The outside world becomes a place where there is the opportunity to interact with others of the same size. Researchers have found that nurturing relationships can develop between very young children with the proper guidance of adults.

Procedures by caregivers that facilitate adjustment

- Strengthen the infant's attachment to the family by cooperating and working closely with parents. Adjustment to child care must never weaken the basic family unit.

- Find out from the parents all you can about the infant, including birth history. What are the child's sleeping habits, eating habits, and patterns of comforting? This communication not only helps you as the caregiver, but also helps parents feel that someone cares about their child.

- Discuss separation procedures. Gradual entry into a new setting, starting with a few hours each day and building to a full day, may make the transition smoother. In the beginning, the parent may stay all the time, then begin leaving for short periods and coming back, demonstrating that he or she does return.

- Sometimes, having the parent leave some personal belonging at the child care setting is reassuring to the infant or toddler. For example, if the mother leaves an extra purse or the father leaves a sweater, the child may be comforted by knowing that the parent will be back for the purse or sweater—and for her too.

- Be sure to say when the parent arrives at the end of each day, "Here's Mother (Father). She (he) came to pick you up after finishing work. That happens every day."

- Understand the parent's point of view. Parents may feel guilty about working and leaving an in-

The very young child may need time to readjust to the parent. Help parents understand that they may not always get an enthusiastic greeting.

preference for the substitute caregiver, but the need for a gradual transition from one person and setting to another.

• Respect and support parents as you help them learn about parenting and how to appreciate and cope with their infants.

• Stagger the admission of new children. Not having all the children start at the same time allows a caregiver to give more individual attention to newcomers. It is easier to add a child to an existing group than to start everyone all at once.

• Recognize that all children are comforted by special objects that are meaningful to them—by their security blankets or teddy bears. Allow and encourage infants and toddlers to bring something to the child care setting that has special meaning for them.

• Be sensitive to the needs of each individual child. A picture of the child's family for the child and the provider to look at together may help. Hearing a parent's voice over the phone could be reassuring to some infants or toddlers who wonder if mother or father has disappeared forever. It could be devastating, however, to a child who has been bravely adjusting to the parent's absence.

• Keep parents informed about what happens during the day but try to *let the parent tell you* how the infant, say, took his first step at home. In other words, let the parent witness the miracle rather than hear how it happened in the child care setting.

• Facilitate friendships among the parents in your group and help them adjust to each other. Parents often feel isolated and need other parents to talk to. Introduce your parents to each other at every opportunity, as you would at a party. Help them get a conversation going. It is very reassuring for parents to talk to other parents with children the same age who are behaving the same way. Potluck dinners for the whole

fant and may be insecure in the parenting role, particularly if this is their first child.

• Help the parent adjust to having a child in child care by working rather than competing with him or her. Explain to the parent that upon being picked up at the end of the day, a young child may need time to readjust to the parent's presence. This does not mean rejection, a lack of love, or a

family and, on occasion, guest speakers talking on a topic of interest are additional ways of encouraging parent-parent interactions.

- Support other caregivers in your center and build cooperative relationships. Positive interactions between adults, a workable adult-child ratio and group size, the chance to discuss and work through problems—all create a climate where the joys of participating in the growth of very young children can outweigh the inherent stresses.

- Provide materials and experiences that match the ever-changing developmental needs of the children. This requires knowledge of age-appropriate activities and an awareness of each child's individual interests and capabilities.

- Facilitate positive interactions among children. Place an infant where she can observe other infants and, as she grows, positively interact with others. This requires constant supervision. The desire to interact and play with others not only supports the adjustment of the infant or toddler but also provides the basis for a lifetime of positive relationships with peers.

- Continue your education and learning by attending classes, inservice presentations, and conferences; reading; analyzing day-to-day experiences with children; and refining observational skills. These promote the professional growth necessary to become an ever-more competent child care provider. By helping parents and infants adjust as smoothly as possible, by caring for themselves and their co-workers, and by matching the child care environment to the individual needs of infants and toddlers, caregivers help everyone benefit from quality infant care.

Reference

National Center for Early Childhood Workforce, 1993. *Child care staffing study revisited: Four years in the life of center-based child care.* Washington, DC: Author.

Chapter 3

Ensuring Health and Safety

Alice Chu

Two major preventable health and safety problems in infant care are infectious diseases and injuries.

Infectious diseases and health risks

The most common problem for infants and toddlers in child care is infectious diseases, ranging in severity from the common cold to bacterial meningitis and various gastrointestinal illnesses. The following suggestions can help prevent infectious disease transmission in child care centers.

Follow basic hygiene practices

1. Wash hands after arriving at the center, changing diapers, wiping an infant's or your own nose, and using the toilet, as well as before handling food (see Appendix A).

2. Wash hands *frequently* with warm, soapy water and dry with disposable towels.

3. Wear disposable gloves for diaper changing (refer to Appendix A). Remove and dispose of gloves after each change. Use bleach solution made daily (1 tablespoon of bleach to 1 quart of water) to disinfect the diapering/changing area after each use. (You will find different bleach formulas in various chapters. Different strengths are used for different purposes.)

4. Separate the diapering area from the food preparation area. The diapering area should be within easy access to a sink.

5. Prepare, label, and store food properly. Disinfect table surfaces and highchair trays after use. Thoroughly wash all cutting surfaces and utensils after each use.

6. Smoke only in designated areas or, better yet, do not smoke.

7. Limit contact with pets; keep them away from food preparation areas.

Limit the number of children in center care to a group size of 8 to 12. A small number of children in a group reduces the incidence of infectious diseases. Separate children who are toilet trained from those who are not.

Make sure there is adequate outdoor time and good ventilation in the facility, as both help control the spread of infection.

Conduct a daily health check as each infant arrives. Isolate any child with a rash, diarrhea, high fever, or skin infection until cleared by a physician.

Inform parents if their infant or toddler has been exposed to a contagious disease so they can be alert to the symptoms of that disease in their child.

Have routine infant health checkups. Routine checkups for infants can detect health problems and ensure that immunizations are administered regularly. Periodic examinations and early diagnosis of

An adult must be able to see each child at all times. Accidents happen as quickly as lightning.

problems can sometimes prevent diseases. Children should be excluded from the child care center whenever they have fevers.

Injuries and accidents

The second preventable common health problem is accidents, including burns, drownings, falls, and choking. Here again, limiting the number of children in center care to a group size of 8 to 12 and maintaining an adult-child ratio of 1:3 are important because these practices allow closer observation and better supervision of children.

Promote a safe physical environment for young children using the following suggestions.

1. Keep all electrical outlets securely covered.

2. Avoid furniture with sharp corners.

3. Provide safe toys (with no small pieces or sharp edges).

4. Use toys that are easily sanitized.

5. Have ample space for children to move in.

6. If a bottle is warmed in a microwave oven, shake it and test the temperature of the milk before feeding an infant.

7. Never use thin plastic material to cover mattresses or pillows.

8. Never tie pacifiers or other items around a baby's neck.

9. During diapering, never leave a baby unattended.

10. Supervise children's activities at all times.

11. Store dangerous and harmful objects and all medicine and household cleaning materials out of children's reach.

12. Rotate responsibilities monthly among the staff for checking for hazardous environmental dangers.

13. Check local guides to identify poisonous plants.

See Appendix B for first aid procedures for some conditions.

Toys for infants and toddlers need to be easily sanitized.

Nutrition

Good nutrition and sound eating habits are essential for proper growth and health. Together, the parent and the provider need to develop a feeding plan before the child's first day in care. The feeding plan will need to be updated frequently as the child's developmental skills progress (see Appendix C). Although the timing and types of foods introduced will follow similar patterns for all children, you should individualize each child's pattern based on developmental needs and pediatrician's recommendations. (See also Appendix D.)

Daily communication, preferably a written report, between parent and provider is needed to ensure consistent feeding practices. You should record what was served, how much was consumed, and any reactions. It is important to introduce new foods one at a time, allowing about one week between foods, to watch for possible allergies.

Mealtimes should be pleasant experiences. Food should never be used to reward or punish children. Hold infants for bottle feedings and talk pleasantly with all children while they are eating.

Feeding babies is more than simply putting nutrients into a baby's body. Feeding a baby should be an intimate and wonderful social interaction between the baby and the caregiver and even, in group infant care, between several babies.

Eating solid food provides opportunities to explore taste and texture, to experiment and explore the consistencies of strained foods and finger foods. It provides opportunities for babies to develop fine motor skills. Speech development also is promoted when a baby is able to explore mouth, teeth, and tongue movement along with chewing and swallowing. Feeding a baby is important for physical health but is equally important for many other aspects of development.

A baby's first introduction to solid foods is typically more important for the experience than for the nutritional value. As babies develop the skills necessary to master eating solid food, the importance of the nutritional value of the food increases proportionately.

Administrative staff responsibilities

(Note: In family child care, the provider is both the administrator and staff.)

First aid and management of minor illnesses

1. Provide staff with inservice training on how to administer first aid and emergency care for such common problems as cuts, bruises, colds, diarrhea, and fever.

2. Provide an adequate first aid kit and a fire extinguisher, both clearly marked and accessible.

3. Update and review with all staff current practices for handling emergency situations as they occur. *In case of an accident or serious health crisis, every adult in the child care setting should know*

Programs for young children need to have written health policies and procedures. No matter how careful we are, children at home and children in care occasionally become ill or injure themselves.

2. Practice emergency procedures frequently at different times of the day. Tell older toddlers it is a game to see how fast everyone can get outside. Do not alarm them.

Health status of staff

1. Before employment, screen staff and volunteers, checking immunization and childhood illness history, to prevent the spread of infectious diseases, chronic diseases, and any other health problems that might affect the children. Every staff member should have a tuberculosis clearance.

2. Supervise, observe, and evaluate staff regarding compliance with sanitation routines.

Health resources

1. Be aware of existing community health resources so staff can make appropriate referrals as needed.

2. Include as health resources local health departments, family physicians, emergency physicians in local hospitals, agencies that provide special health services, and police and fire rescue teams.

under what circumstances to call the emergency number 911 to summon paramedics. Any life-threatening situation such as breathing problems, excessive bleeding, or difficulty moving that the caregiver does not know how to treat requires the immediate attention of medical personnel. (See also Appendix B.)

4. Require cardiopulmonary resuscitation (CPR) training for all staff every two years.

Evacuation, emergency, and disaster plans

1. Visibly post emergency plans and evacuation procedures to follow in the event of fire, flood, earthquake, and other emergencies.

3. Consider indoor pollution hazards such as asbestos, pesticides, lead, and household chemicals. Check with federal agencies such as the Consumer Product Safety Commission (800-638-2772) and the Environmental Protection Agency for information and updates on hazards to children.

4. Call your local health department whenever your program has two or more cases of the same communicable disease.

Health records

It is a good idea to encourage open channels of communication with the infant's pediatrician from the start. One excellent approach to this, practiced by a center in the Los Angeles area, is to send a form letter and brochure to each child's pediatrician when the child registers at the center. The brochure (or duplicated information about the center) informs the pediatrician of the center's philosophy and general policies and invites her or him to get in touch with the center regarding comments, questions, or suggestions for special precautions to safeguard the health of the particular infant. Although responses from pediatricians should not be expected at that time, this initial outreach makes it easier to communicate with them if the need arises.

1. Maintain complete, regularly updated health records for each child. Records should include health history, immunizations, screening tests, allergies, and other physical limitations, and the name, address, and phone number of the child's physician.

2. Update parents' or guardians' home and work addresses and phone numbers every six months.

3. Include the phone numbers of at least two additional people to contact in case of emergency.

4. Obtain from the parent or legal guardian a signed consent form to be used for emergency medical treatment.

Health policies and procedures

Written policies and procedures facilitate staff and parent compliance. Staff and parents should sign a form stating that they understand the health policies of the infant care program. Assign qualified staff to serve as liaison between the center and the child's parents or guardians. Terms of the health policy should cover

1. management of injuries and acute illnesses, including exclusion policies

2. regulations regarding the administration of medications (see Appendix F for permission form)

3. the handling of food and formulas and the care of breast-fed babies

4. bathing, if facilities are available

5. napping arrangements, including care of linen

6. emergency plans

7. expected involvement and participation of parents in health matters

When parents leave their babies in our care they have a right to know that we are taking every common sense precaution to keep the children healthy and safe. It is the least we should do.

Supporting Breast Feeding and Working Mothers

The American Academy of Pediatrics now recognizes breastfeeding as the superior method of feeding babies for at least the first six months. Unfortunately, in the United States the rate of maternal breastfeeding has actually decreased over the last 20 years. And, an academy study indicates that although most women who are planning to reenter the workforce after the birth of their babies intend to breastfeed, only 20% of them actually do so longer than six weeks after they go back to work.

Infant caregivers are in a unique position to support working mothers. Breast milk is a remarkable food for babies, especially for those in group care situations. Not only does the child receive the antibodies that the mother has developed and passed on through her milk, but when a baby is exposed to specific germs and then breastfeeds, the breast responds by producing antibodies specific to the disease to which the child has been exposed. This, in combination with the nutritional aspects of the milk, makes breastfeeding well worth any slight inconveniences to the mother or the caregivers.

Storage and preparation of expressed breast milk

Mothers can express milk manually using hand, electric, or battery-operated pumps. This milk can be kept refrigerated for up to two days and frozen in a conventional freezer for up to two weeks, with a zero-degree freezer allowing storage of up to three months.

Milk should be warmed slowly by immersing the container in warm water (a slow cooker set on low and filled with water works well). *Under no circumstances should breast milk be microwaved.* Not only are there very strong possibilities of hot spots that could cause burning, but breast milk is relatively unstable and can lose its nutrients during the microwaving process. Warmed breast milk can be transferred to the bottle of the baby's choice.

Bottle feeding

Babies who have been breastfed from birth frequently do not immediately know how to suck from an artificial nipple. They may turn their head and protest vigorously when offered a bottle, even when hungry. When possible, a new mother can give someone else her expressed breast milk to feed to the newborn in a bottle. This may still result in resistance later on, but it will give caregivers an extra edge in teaching newborns how to suck from an artificial nipple. A first introduction to a bottle is usually best handled by someone other than the mother and is best received if the bottle contains breast milk.

A baby who refuses to take a bottle can be induced to do so by a patient and persistent caregiver. Holding the bottle away from the body and turning the baby away from the caregiver, plus walking or movement, usually with a drowsy baby, can get the baby to suck and be rewarded without being confused by the expectation that he or she is about to nurse. This can take several tenacious feedings daily for a week or more, so don't get discouraged. In the meantime, if liquid intake is of concern, liquid can be dribbled into the baby's mouth with a spoon. When trying to encourage a baby to take a bottle, have several styles of bottles and nipples to offer. Some babies have a decided preference for one style or another. The orthodontic style and natural style seem to work well for many babies.

Offering support

For the mother

Mothers who choose to combine working and breastfeeding need lots of support and help. They may feel guilty because they have been unsuccessful at getting their baby to take a bottle at home. They may be pressured at work not to take the time to express milk or to leave the office to feed their baby in the middle of the day. Since a baby who is healthy and can fight infections well is a definite advantage in any group care situation, it is to the caregiver's benefit as well as to the baby's and mother's to help a mother through these difficulties.

Mothers who are breastfeeding also have the additional complication that the hormones released during the process of feeding their baby are also those that stimulate maternal feelings and can make separating from their child more difficult. Acknowledging the mother's feelings as normal can help the mother through the process.

That enforced time of quiet while feeding a baby after a long day's work can really help a mother switch from her professional life to her personal one in a positive way. The reunion process is a peaceful and intimate one in a way that bottle feeding may not be.

For the baby

Breast milk is more easily digested than formula. Because of this, babies who are being breastfed tend to need to eat more frequently than those who are just receiving formula. Caregivers must respond to this need by offering bottles more frequently. Small amounts of breast milk can be warmed more often.

Keeping a bottle of water available also can help. If a baby is acting hungry and the mother is due to come and feed within 45 minutes or so, a little bit of warm water can stave off hunger pains without filling up the baby. Some mothers may choose to offer supplemental formula. If the baby is resisting this option but doing well with bottles in general, suggest that the formula be mixed with breast milk in gradually decreasing amounts until the baby accepts the formula.

Professional services

Caregivers can assist breastfeeding mothers by being in touch with local lactation consultants and by referring mothers to these educators when problems or difficulties arise. Lactation consultation is now available in most areas. Consultants and breastfeeding educators are specially trained to help mothers with problems or difficulties associated with breastfeeding. They can give advice about milk expression, choices of breast pumps, sore breasts and nipples, engorgement, or breastfeeding babies with special needs. They also are trained to help a mother develop a special plan to succeed in breastfeeding while she is working. Check your local *Yellow Pages* or ask local obstetricians about a lactation consultant. The local La Leche League also may have sources for help and support.

Although breastfeeding and working may take some additional effort and attention, it is well worthwhile to all parties involved. The feeling of satisfaction that a caregiver gets when seeing a healthy mother and baby together is beyond measure.

— *Bobbie Edwards*

Chapter 4

Providing Learning and Growth Experiences for Children

Rose Bromwich

Continuity of care

Each infant should receive continuous care by the same one or two adults, or by as few adults as possible (especially during the first 12 to 15 months of life). These individuals will be referred to here as the *significant adults* in the child's life in the child care setting.

A limited number of significant adults for each child is important so that

- the child can form secure attachments (the child builds trust in a few—not all—adults);
- the caregiver can form a bond, thus stimulating an interest in the growth and achievement of each individual infant and enhancing his ability to sustain quality interactions throughout the months of routine caregiving;
- adults who know the child well and see him for extended periods every day will know what is "normal" for that child with respect to physical signs of health or illness (such as skin color, body temperature, and stool consistency, color, and frequency) and with respect to emotional signs such as mood, common social reactions, and emotional tone; and
- the caregiver knows each individual infant's developmental achievement level and personal learning style and what works to motivate him or her.

At no time should any infant or young child be out of the sight or hearing of at least one adult. Each significant adult should try to understand what a child's behavior might mean for that particular child at that particular time. Each child has a different makeup that affects behavior and reactions as much as it does physical appearance. For example, some children seem especially "tough" or resilient, and others seem especially sensitive or vulnerable. Care providers who have this awareness will not come to a group of young children with set ideas of how all infants or all 2-year-olds should act or be responded to, treated, or "trained."

Adult-child interactions

The significant adult should engage in considerable interaction with the child during *caretaking* activities such as feeding, bathing, and diapering. The child is conscious of being with the significant adult. We should not view caretaking time (time when the significant adult *has* to be with the child) as something to get over with as quickly as possible but as an opportunity to foster healthy development through pleasurable adult-infant interactions. Caretaking time offers great opportunities to smile at, talk to, make eye contact with, and even engage in social games with the child. This is especially important for the younger infant, whose range of activities with the significant adult is more limited than that of older infants and toddlers.

With very young infants, adults must be sensitive to different tolerance levels—to the amount of stimulation each child can handle and profit from. Sometimes crying and fussing can result from overstimulation. When an adult engages in physical play with an infant who is not yet mobile, the adult should carefully observe the infant's cues regarding what the baby enjoys without showing signs of fear. Great care should be taken not to engage the young infant in vigorous movements (such as throwing) that may shake the infant's head in a forward and backward motion. This whiplash effect is dangerous; severe damage to an infant's spine can result from well-meant but too-rough physical play.

Here are some suggestions for interactions with infants who are not yet mobile.

1. Position the child to permit a wide range of vision and a variety of interesting sights.
2. Put the infant into positions that allow free movement of arms and hands and therefore facilitate the manipulation of materials.
3. Provide safe and sufficient space for each child to move and play.
4. Remove materials not currently of interest to the infant.

Caretaking time should by no means be the only time the significant adult interacts with infants. Interactions with adults are important for children's emotional health and social, language, and cognitive development. Each child should

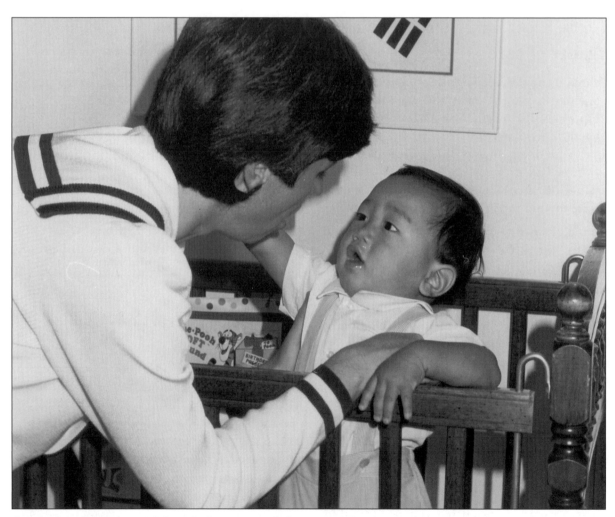

Continuity of care is crucial. To feel secure, an infant or toddler must develop a friendship with one or two "significant adults."

have opportunities for the following experiences many times a day:

- frequent eye contact and social interaction with the significant adult who makes special time" to be with the infant.

- affectionate holding when the child seems to want or welcome it. It is also important to let the child go when she seems ready (by giving behavioral cues) to leave the adult. Holding the child against her will, even when the significant adult means to be affectionate, may interfere with the child's trust in the caregiver's ability to read and respond to her cues.

- interaction with the significant adult in a manner that establishes a kind of "conversation" or reciprocity between the child and the adult. This is important even before the child does much vocalizing in social interactions. Be aware that when the infant looks attentively at a person's face, she is responding to that person and his or her language.

- allowing the infant opportunities to *respond* to the adult, even though that response may be internal and not observable. Observable aspects of an internal response by the infant may include stopping activity, quieting, and intense looking at the adult's face. By 3 months of age, often soon after reaching 1 month, the child responds to social play with a smile or a laugh.

Within the context of pleasurable, satisfying interactions with significant people in his environment, the infant's language—wanting to listen and communicate—gradually develops. Language/communication should be pleasurable for the child. A few specific activities for the significant adult to use with the infant to foster language are given here.

1. Respond vocally or verbally to the child's sounds, gestures, and movements. (Later, respond to the child's vocalizations and, still later, to the child's verbal language, including jargon.)

2. Talk, sing, or hum to the baby, even when he does not give a vocal response.

3. Talk to the child about what he hears, feels, and does. (Be sure to pause so as not to overwhelm the child with speech.) This helps connect language with experiences.

4. Give the child time and opportunities to communicate his needs and wants; do not always assume that you know them. (Caution: Do not force the child to verbalize if there is resistance.)

5. Make pictures and books a part of the infant's experience. Talk about what you think she might be looking at in the picture and respond to her pointing at objects. Encourage gesturing and vocalizing.

6. Learn a few common phrases in the child's home language. (See Appendix E for toddler vocabulary in Spanish, French, Hebrew, and Farsi.)

Infant-infant interactions

When the same children are frequently together, they become increasingly interested in each other. The intensity of that interest varies from child to child and from one moment to another, and generally increases with age. Anyone who has seen twin infants or baby cousins "play" together knows that a form of friendship is possible—and even quite likely—very early in life. A few group activities, such as music time, help infants become aware not only of each other but also, gradually, of themselves and of others as part of a group.

When one infant is interested in exploring or "playing with" another infant and the second baby shows more interest in playing with a toy rather than with a friend, the child's independent play should be respected.

Infants are not aware of what hurts another child and what does not as they explore each other. Therefore, adults should carefully observe infants' interactions, support positive contacts, and intervene in any actions that might hurt or injure.

Play and the infant's development

The play of infants and young children is not "just" play. It is a basic need, not only for intellectual growth but also for social, emotional, and motor (fine- and gross-motor) development. The child's involvement in activities with *interesting* objects—that is, what is interesting to that child at that particular time—nurtures one of the most important natural incentives for growth in the

Even babies develop friendship among themselves. They enjoy each other's company and benefit from it.

child: interest and motivation to explore, experiment with, and problem solve with a variety of materials.

When a child's interest in objects and in people in the world around her is not stimulated, one of her major needs is not being met. Children who do not have opportunities to become engaged with a variety of materials at their individual levels of skill and to choose their own goals in those activities tend to become increasingly passive, angry, and aggressive, or just unhappy as a result of boredom. They tend to function nowhere near their social, emotional, and intellectual potential. When we do not capitalize on children's natural curiosity or interest we may stunt their social, emotional, and intellectual growth.

Psychosocial (affective) development and cognitive (intellectual) development are inseparable in the infant and young child. The child who is emotionally healthy—who is attached to and trusts significant adults in the home and child care setting—usually will be motivated to explore his physical environment. Part of that physical environment is objects that become play materials.

Consult books in our annotated bibliography for ideas on activities at different developmental levels. But first and foremost, observe each individual child. The child herself will tell you, through her behavior and by her own way of acting on objects, what she is ready for and what interests her at a particular time. Some suggestions for play materials are offered here.

1. With individual interests in mind, make a variety of materials available to the infant or toddler at his or her developmental level.

2. Make available play materials that are responsive to the child's actions (those that reveal cause and effect).

3. Create interesting and varied opportunities for activities that use different sense modalities (vision, hearing, touch, smell, and taste).

4. Provide ample opportunity and sufficient time and space for each child to engage with interesting materials. The materials (not necessarily commercial toys) should be challenging but also should ensure success—that is, they should not cause frustration.

5. When interacting with a child during play, be aware of the child's tempo and pace your interaction accordingly.

6. Break down elements of an activity that the child chooses according to the child's developmental level—for example, hand pegs for a peg board to the child one at a time—to help ensure success in play.

7. Encourage, help, or redirect the child when he has difficulty achieving his goal in play.

8. Introduce materials to a child based on your observations of his success with materials requiring the same or similar skills.

9. In symbolic or dramatic play, let the child direct *you* with respect to the role he wants you to play.

Fine-motor development takes care of itself when developmentally appropriate play materials are available. For gross-motor activity, children need space and equipment that allow them to engage safely in vigorous physical play, both indoors and outdoors. The relative level of gross-motor activity varies greatly among infants and young children. Interest in physically vigorous play tends to be more intense at some periods in a child's development than at others. Toddlers do not always know what they can execute safely, and they need close supervision in gross-motor activities.

It is important to provide ample opportunity for all the infants and toddlers in a child care setting to engage in as much gross-motor activity as they seem to desire. Occasionally it may be appropriate to encourage a very sedentary child to attempt something new and challenging, but remember that not all infants and children need the same amount of physical exercise.

Play activity in infant and child care settings is important for all children but especially for those who do not get much stimulation in language and play in their homes.

Recognizing developmental progress and delay

Among behaviors that can be observed in the normally developing infant within the first four months or so of life are

- making and maintaining eye contact with a person for more than an instant;

- focusing and maintaining attention on an object and visually following it across the midline of the body;

- holding head up at a 45- to 90-degree angle when on abdomen in a prone position; and

- showing evidence of social responsiveness, culminating in that smile that parents often eagerly anticipate.

Signs indicating further observation or consultation/referral

A few behavioral signs are mentioned here that suggest the need for further observation of the infant's behavior in all developmental areas. If these signs of possible problems persist, *consultation with or referral to a child development professional or a developmental pediatrician might be advisable.*

It is important for parents and providers to calculate the adjusted age of any infant born preterm, beginning from the expected date of birth (term date) rather than from the day the infant actually was born. If developmental delays should occur, even considering the child's adjusted age, they usually can be observed in the second half of the first year of life, by around 9 or 10 months of age.

The least reliable signs of possible delay are late walking or late talking, because wide variations occur within normal development in both these areas. However, if more than two of the following behaviors persist, there may be a delay in one or more developmental areas.

At 4 or so months, a baby can make and maintain eye contact for more than an instant.

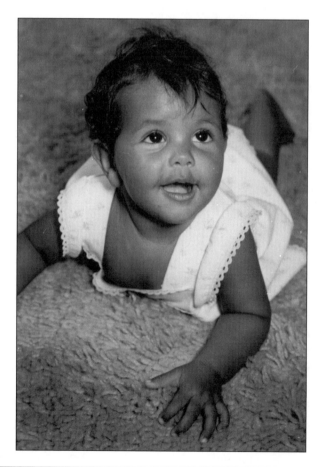

Holding the head up at a 45- to 90-degree angle is normal for an infant within the first 4 months or so of life.

*Small babies can show social responsiveness—
including that special smile eagerly anticipated
by parents—by the fourth month or so.*

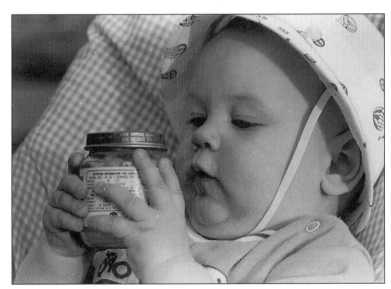

*An infant, usually within the first 4 months of life,
can focus and maintain attention on an object.*

At 10 months (or adjusted age for the preterm infant), the infant

- does not sit independently;

- does not transfer objects from one hand to the other, crossing the midline;

- does not discriminate between parent and other adults;

- makes few language sounds (vocalizations)—sounds limited to fussing and crying;

- shows limited or no interest in objects and toys; and

- does not yet mouth objects.

At 12 months (or adjusted age for the preterm infant), the infant

- does not search for an object or toy of great interest when an adult suddenly covers it with a cloth (looking for hidden objects shows evidence of *object permanence*, or the child's awareness that an object still exists after it disappears from sight—an important milestone of normal cognitive development);

- does not pick up crumbs or cereal with thumb and index or middle finger; and

- does not focus on a picture of a familiar object or animal in a book.

In addition to these behaviors, certain other signs that indicate possible sensory or motor problems can be observed easily in an infant care setting. Some of the following signs may be observed earlier than 9 or 10 months.

Possible visual problems exist if the infant

- does not make eye contact with others or holds objects closer than three or four inches from one or both eyes; and

- does not reach for an object close by.

Possible hearing problems exist if the infant

- does not respond to sounds or to the voices of familiar people; and

- does not attend to bells or other sound-producing objects.

Excessively high muscle tone may exist if the infant

- has limbs that are stiff and feel tight; and

- stands early and supports her own weight by maintaining a standing position rigidly without knees flexing periodically (parents may be pleased that the child is eager to stand for long periods, but the infant *may not be able to move* out of the rigid standing position).

Excessively low muscle tone may exist if the infant

- has floppy limbs;

- feels limp when picked up; and

- cannot sustain his own weight, even for a brief moment, at 10 or 11 months.

Abnormally high or low muscle tone may or may not be related to possible neurological problems. Possible visual, auditory, or muscle-tone problems should be checked by the infant's pediatrician.

Some additional worrisome behaviors in *toddlers* are when the child

- shows dramatic changes in behavior, from age appropriate to age inappropriate or deviant, that last for several weeks (for example, he rocks and bangs self rhythmically over and over, produces continuous unpleasant, nonlanguage sounds not directed toward anyone in particular, or engages in long uninterrupted screaming *without apparent cause*); and

- stops vocalizing and/or talking, and the previous language skill does not return for several weeks.

In cases where such behaviors are observed for long periods, you should confer with the parents and refer them to the child's pediatrician, a child guidance clinic, or a child psychiatrist or psychologist.

If any infant shows behavior such as lack of eye contact, flat affect (lack of any emotional reaction or expression or social response), or little or no interest in becoming engaged with people or even with object, the infant should be observed further in interaction with a provider. Increase your contact with the infant's parents, including scheduling a home visit and/or an individual conference.

Every infant needs to have the opportunity to develop a close relationship with one or two providers.

If the infant's behavior and seemingly depressed state cannot be explained by particular crises in the infant's life, such as recent hospitalization or separation from the primary caregiver/parent, find out more about the interactions and relationhips between the infant and parent or others in the home.

If the infant has not developed an emotional attachment to anyone at home, it is important to explore the possible reasons. Is the family or the parent currently under severe stress? Who is the primary caregiver in the home, and in what mental/emotional state is this person? Is she or he in a position to provide sufficient nurturing or even basic care for the infant, or is intervention and/or referral needed?

Every effort should be made to enable the infant to develop a close relationship with and trust in one or two providers who particularly like the infant. In cases where highly abnormal or pathological interactions are found between parent and infant, the parent should be referred for help as soon as possible. Child guidance clinics or specific family stress centers are good resources for these kinds of problems.

According to law, child protective services must be contacted whenever a situation arises that puts the infant or other children in the home in immediate danger. Body bruises or signs of sexual abuse in the genital or rectal region must be reported immediately and carefully noted with time and date in the caregiver's log book (it might be required later as evidence).

Chapter 5

Caring for Children with Special Needs

Rose Bromwich and Harriet Kleinman

Child care providers may worry about some issues in out-of-home care for infants with disabilities or babies born at high risk. Among the questions that may arise are these:

- How safe is it for the infant to be in child care, whether it be in a child care center or in a family child care home?

- How much extra time will infants with certain special needs require?

- Does the provider know enough about these infants to be able to care for them adequately?

- What impact will the presence of certain children with special needs have on the other children and their parents?

The purpose of this chapter is to provide information and some background on infants and young children with various special needs. Such information should help caregivers answer some of these questions as well as learn how to obtain needed information regarding any particular child or situation.

This chapter is divided into three major sections. Section 1 addresses issues regarding infants born with disabilities and those who are medically at risk for continuing problems or disabilities. Section 2 discusses the needs of infants whose environment puts them at risk for problems or disabilities. It also addresses issues regarding infants at biological *and* environmental risk, a category that includes infants prenatally exposed to drugs (a biological factor).

Although prenatally drug-exposed infants are considered to be biologically at risk for continuing problems, the severity of the risk varies from minimal to serious. Unfortunately, these vulnerable infants frequently are born into home environments that present an even higher risk of problems. Section 3 discusses some of the potential benefits of out-of-home care for infants with special needs.

1. Infants with disabilities or born at risk for disabilities

Information on each individual infant, whether she has a disability or is at risk for disabilities, is usually available both from the parents and from the child's pediatrician or specialist. These persons are able to provide information on whether a particular infant needs special care and, if so, what kind of care and extra attention she may need. The parent or professional also is able to tell the care provider what specific problems are connected with the infant's at-risk status or disabling condition.

Infants born with disabilities

Some infants are born with chromosomal abnormalities. Only a few of the most common ones will be discussed here. The most frequently occurring of these conditions is Down's syndrome. Other infants are born with sensory impairments in the areas of vision and hearing. Another disability that can usually be diagnosed at or before 9 months of age is cerebral palsy, a condition caused by neurological damage. Each of these disabilities can exist in isolation from or in combination with other problems.

The mental ability of infants with Down's syndrome ranges from mildly to severely retarded. Some also may have heart disease or other medical problems. These infants are known for their sociability and easy temperament.

Infants with sensory impairments or cerebral palsy and who were very early preemies (born 12 to 17 weeks preterm) or who suffered considerable damage at birth may have additional disabilities or health problems. Sensory impairments or cerebral palsy can occur without other problems, however. Many children with cerebral palsy are intellectually normal or may even be gifted. Although it is common knowledge that children with normal intellectual potential can have hearing or visual impairment, it is not widely known that the same can be true of a child with cerebral palsy. The following quotation from a respected researcher in special education makes this point clear:

> There is actually little direct relation between intelligence and degree of physical impairment in cerebral palsy. A person with severe writhing or uncontrolled spasticity may be intellectually gifted while one with mild, almost unnoticed involvement may be severely mentally retarded. (Kirk 1972, 359–60)

According to the same author, approximately 50% of children with cerebral palsy fall within the normal range of intelligence. The children with cerebral palsy who also are retarded, mildly or severely, suffered damage to more extensive areas of the brain. It is often difficult to predict, much before age 3, whether a severely motorically involved child has normal (or above) intellectual capacity. Assessments of development in the cognitive (intellectual) and language areas before age 2 rely largely on the child's performance in areas that require fine-motor activity of hands and mouth (for speech).

Some children are born with visible anomalies such as limb deficiencies. The most common upper-extremity congenital deficiency is one arm that ends just below the elbow. Infants born with this condition adapt naturally and amazingly well to the absence of forearm and hand, and they usually have no problem engaging in most activities expected at their age. Infants with this type of anomaly should do well in infant care; they need little extra attention from the child care provider. There is no reason to exclude these children from either family child care or center-based care. In fact, such children are a positive example of the amazing physical adaptability that human beings demonstrate, especially early in life. The same applies to children with other limb deficiencies.

It is the parents' decision whether or not a particular child will have a prosthesis, or terminal device. The child will do well either way. If the parents favor a prosthesis (there are several types), it is usually provided sometime during the last half of the first year of life. At this age, the prosthesis is not functional, but a passive device is introduced and worn early to help the infant get used to it as part of his or her body. Sometime between 18 and 24 months, the child is fitted with an active terminal device and is taught, by specialists in this area, how to use it.

Some children wear the prosthesis only some of the time. Some do not want to wear it at all. It is important for these children's attitude toward themselves and their own bodies, with or without the terminal device, to be accepted; child care providers should not put pressure on a child to wear the device. The young child's adaptability with and without a prosthesis is usually quite remarkable.

Infants biologically at risk for disabilities

Most infants identified as medically or biologically at risk are those born preterm, whose gestational age (age from conception) at the time of birth was considerably less than 37 to 40 weeks. This population has grown substantially in the last two decades, mainly because of rapidly advancing medical technology that enables infants born as early as 23 weeks' gestational age to be kept alive. Infants born between 23 and 27 weeks' gestational age (sometimes referred to as very preterm) usually are put on respirators because their respiratory system is too immature to sustain life. Unfortunately, the amount and pressure of the oxygen necessary for their survival may put their vision at risk. Furthermore, infants who remain on a respirator for two months or longer are prone to bronchopulmonary displagia (BPD), a weakness

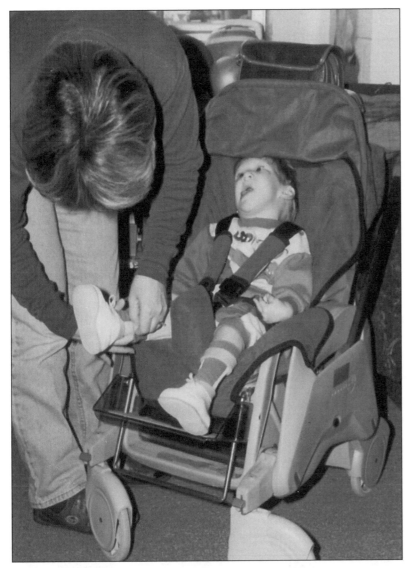

Sensory impairments or cerebral palsy can occur without additional disabilities or health problems.

infants are more likely to be born preterm and to be at medical risk for a number of reasons. These very young teenage girls are less likely to carry a fetus to full term. Also, many of these "children having children" do not seek or get prenatal care, nor are they apt to follow the nutritional regimen needed by a pregnant female to bear a healthy, full-term infant.

There is another group of biologically high-risk infants, one that has grown at an alarming rate in the last decade: infants prenatally exposed to drugs. Women who take street drugs (often multiple drugs) are most prevalent in poor urban areas. Prenatal exposure to considerable amounts of alcohol can be devastating to infants (causing fetal alcohol syndrome). Because both environmental and biological risks are present for most drug-exposed infants, relevant information is provided separately in the next section.

2. Infants at environmental risk

The number of infants at risk due to environmental factors also has been growing. Some of the conditions causing stress on parents may be chronic, such as poverty and crime-ridden neighborhoods; others may be temporary but intense in their effect on the parent or primary caregiver. Many stresses that families experience are interrelated—for example, poverty, job loss, part-time or temporary employment with low pay, lack of functional support system, and relationship problems.

Patterns of neglect and abuse are not uncommon in such families—neglect because of concerns about and preoccupations with other matters, at least temporarily; abuse often arising from frustration and displaced anger. These parental behavior patterns are more likely to exist when the parent is under severe stress as a result of the simultaneous occurrence of multiple events.

Teenage mothers and older single mothers without adequate support systems also are subjected to a great deal of stress and, it appears, diminishing support from society (as of the end of 1995). Hav-

and vulnerability of the lungs that may continue into the preschool years.

During the first few months after hospital discharge, many infants born preterm may give less clear signals or cues than other infants, and they may be fussier. Some may have softer, higher-pitched cries, show more irregular sleep patterns, and take longer to feed. Very preterm and sick infants who had prolonged respiratory distress syndrome (RDS) and developed BPD are usually more susceptible to colds and other respiratory infections.

Another factor that has caused an increase in the number of infants born biologically at risk for disabilities is the increasing number of births by 11- to 15-year-old teens (hardly any increase has occurred in births to girls between ages 16 and 19). Their

ing their infants in quality child care (a family child care home or center)—knowing that their children are safe and in a physically and mentally healthy environment and sensing that the care providers also care about them, as very young mothers—provides much-needed support for these women.

Some mothers who are mentally retarded (developmentally disabled) put their infants and children at risk for serious problems and disabilities due to their own disabilities, which may co-exist with psychiatric disorders. Such parents may be so preoccupied with themselves and their own needs that they are not able to attend to and meet the needs of their infants and children.

Most mothers with such problems and disabilities, as well as some other parents, have been characterized as "psychologically (or emotionally) unavailable." Longitudinal research on their children at the University of Minnesota has found that

The psychological unavailability pattern [of mothers] was particularly devastating [more so than other forms of neglect or physical abuse] to the child's development. The sharp decline in the intellectual functioning of these children, their attachment disturbances and subsequent lack of social/emotional competence in a variety of situations is cause for great concern. (Egeland & Erickson 1987, 115)

The infants in the families described here are certainly at risk for neglect and/or abuse, for developmental delays and disabilities, as well as psychological problems.

Infants environmentally and biologically at risk

As might be expected, when infants are at double risk, biologically and environmentally, they also are doubly vulnerable and have a much poorer prognosis than if the risk factors were only medical or only environmental in nature. As Rutter (1981) points out,

In good social conditions the disadvantage [of low birthweight infants—not those born 12 to 17 weeks preterm or those with neurological damage] is negligible or nonexistent, but there seems to be an interaction effect so that the effects of low birthweight are greatest in deprived social circumstances. The biological handicap acts by lowering the organism's adaptability and increasing its vulnerability to environmental hazard. (p. 100)

Research has repeatedly confirmed that biologically at-risk infants are especially vulnerable to detrimental environmental factors. In fact, low birthweight and perinatal complications without

Young children with special needs benefit from social interactions with typically developing children.

Part I: Considerations in Infant and Toddler Care

neurological damage have not been found to be predictive of continuing problems in childhood except when combined with home environment factors such as low-quality caregiving and poor mother-infant interaction (Bromwich 1985).

Unfortunately, the majority of biologically vulnerable (or at-risk) infants are born into families who further put the infant at environmental risk. Factors contributing to a preterm birth include poor nutrition and minimal or no pre-natal care of the mother. Conditions stressful to the mother, such as poverty, lack of a support system, inadequate housing, and an unsafe neighborhood, may worsen a pregnant woman's feelings of depression or hopelessness. This state of mind often leads her to neglect her own health and makes her more likely to disregard medical advice for proper self-care. In fact, many women living in poverty may not get sufficient rest, and many teenagers do not seek medical care prior to the baby's birth. All these factors, singly or in combination with each other, can contribute to inadequate fetal growth and premature birth. In contrast, infants born with disabilities are more equally distributed across all populations.

Another infant population exposed to both biological and environmental risk factors is the prenatally drug-exposed infant. The number of these infants has increased particularly in poor urban areas. Because so much is now known about ways to support the development of these infants, this population deserves a separate section.

Prenatally drug-exposed infants

A case can be made that almost all infants prenatally exposed to drugs or alcohol are born into families—families in all socio-economic strata—that also put them at environmental risk.

An addicted mother is primarily concerned about herself and has very poor prospects for adequately addressing her infant's needs. However, the same mother might fight vigorously in court when faced with the loss of authority over her child. Because of overwhelmed foster care systems and strong family reunification policies, substance-abusing mothers

Children with a variety of disabilities can profit from good, developmental infant/toddler programs.

frequently succeed in preserving parental rights. It is not unusual for a drug-abusing mother to slip through a hospital toxic-substance screen or return to drug use after completing a rehabilitation program. Infants are sometimes placed with relatives who themselves are not equipped to cope with the special needs of a prenatally drug-exposed child. These biologically vulnerable children often just find themselves in another precarious environment.

Prenatal drug exposure implies greater risk for sudden infant death syndrome (SIDS), retarded growth (in utero and aggravated by poor feeding), and vision and hearing difficulties. Due to her lifestyle, a drug-abusing mother is more likely to pass on gonorrhea, syphilis, herpes, hepatitis, or HIV infection to her child. Fetal alcohol syndrome (FAS) with mental retardation may occur in conjunction with other problems. Cocaine use is known to trigger labor, thereby adding risks associated with premature birth (Tyler 1990).

Early symptoms. The medical problems and behavioral manifestations of these babies can be so taxing that even highly motivated foster parents or guardians can be quickly drained. For example, in the neonatal "withdrawal" period, infants prenatally exposed to narcotics may exhibit

• *central nervous system symptoms:* high-pitched cry, prolonged crying, abnormal (very short) sleep patterns, jitteriness, tremors, muscle-tone problems (stiffness), seizures, fever

Provide lots of interactions that include touching, eye contact, and talking.

- *gastrointestinal symptoms:* poor feeding with frequent regurgitation, frantic fist sucking, vomiting, diarrhea, dehydration

- *vasomotor symptoms:* sweating, nasal stuffiness, mottling

- *skin problem:* abrasions from constant rubbing against bedding. (Merker, Higgins, & Kinnard 1985)

In addition, cocaine-exposed infants are characterized by extreme lethargy and low tone, alternating with bouts of extreme irritability. PCP exposure also may involve staring or unusual eye movements (Tyler 1990).

Continuing risks. Some symptoms may not appear until after a child is discharged from the hospital and the caregiver begins to observe abnormal signs. Beyond the extreme problems of withdrawal already noted and problems of prematurity, which normally would be treated in a neonatal intensive care unit, a constellation of behavioral symptoms are likely to be first noted by caregivers of babies who were prenatally drug-exposed. Symptoms may include poor feeding and sleeping patterns; hypersensitivity or hyperirritability; difficulty in consoling self and in being comforted; increased tone and tremors; decreased quality of movement; poor organization of behavior; behavioral extremes; poor control of states of alertness; decreased focused attention; depressed interactive behaviors; decreased use of adults for so-

lace, play, and object attainment; and problems with separation and attachment (Poulsen 1991).

Anyone, especially a mother with a drug-abuse history, can be stressed to a breaking point trying to provide care to such a vulnerable child with so many special needs. Practical, educational, and emotional support can be helpful, but addicted mothers seldom have an effective support system, and funded sources of respite are a rarity. High risk for abuse and neglect is a reality in this population.

If funding were available and the infant or toddler not too medically fragile for a group setting, several positive outcomes could accrue from out-of-home child care. For example, a "borderline" mother may be able to function reasonably well with daytime respite and the opportunity to earn a living. Meanwhile, a highly responsive child care environment may provide an ameliorating situation for an at-risk child. Many benefits that apply to other infants with special needs, discussed in the following section, apply to these children as well.

The outcome of prenatal drug exposure in infants can range from normality, to subtle behavioral abnormalities, to various degrees of developmental delay and social-emotional difficulties. Therefore, the term *drug-exposed children* should not be used as a label with the assumption that these children's problems are necessarily similar either in degree or in kind. Many factors are involved, and answers are limited, even to such basic questions as "What drug(s) did the mother use during her pregnancy?" (Most drug abusers are multidrug users, do not give accurate histories, and tend to avoid being questioned at all; plus, drug-screen tests are notoriously unreliable.) In addition, a multiplicity of complications may or may not occur. Clearly, there is no uniformity of outcome.

For many of these children, quality care, as emphasized throughout this book, is essential. Just as is true among infants generally, some drug-exposed infants are easier to care for than others; individuality among drug-exposed children should be respected as much as in the general population. Nonetheless, some suggestions can be offered for making the care of symptomatic babies more rewarding.

Quality care

Feeding

1. Swaddle and hold the infant during feeding. Avoid propped bottles.

2. Use bottles only for feeding liquids. Use a spoon for solids.

3. For a particular infant experiencing feeding problems, seek advice from the infant's pediatrician on starting solid foods and juices.

4. Burp babies frequently. For some babies, burp after each ounce of fluid.

5. Feed in a quiet place away from distractions. Avoid sudden movements.

6. Allow more time for feeding unusually sleepy babies. Encourage them to stay awake by massaging the back, rubbing the soles, and talking.

7. Guard against overfeeding (an intense need to suck can camouflage a full stomach; try a pacifier).

Comforting

1. Swaddle with the baby's hands exposed.

2. Walk and hold the baby close; use a front carrier.

3. Bathe the baby in warm water and follow with gentle massage.

4. Lie on your back and place the infant on your chest face down. Gently massage the baby's back.

5. Offer a pacifier.

6. Speak softly.

7. Gently rock the infant in a wind-up cradle or swing (with good head support).

8. Try soft music in a quiet room; avoid bright lights, jostling, and loud noises.

Adapted from *Special Care for Special Babies*, pamphlet developed by UCLA Intervention Program, Judy Howard, director, through Grant #024 AH 50027 (n.d.), U.S. Department of Education, Handicapped Children in Early Education Programs.

Other risk factors

Additional problems

As the infant grows older, other risk factors may become apparent. Some traits and behaviors point to poor attachment and sense of self.

1. Decreased use of adults for solace, play, and object attainment and conflict resolution
2. Indiscriminant attachment to strangers
3. Low demand for and response to praise
4. Low response to verbal direction
5. Regressive behavior
6. Difficulty in making choices
7. Delayed imitation behavior, language, and symbolic play
8. Low task persistence
9. Increased tantrums and oppositional behavior when faced with difficult tasks
10. Low self-dependence in daily living skills
11. Avoidance of new challenges
12. Increased clinging to adults
13. Decreased empathy and prosocial behaviors

Developing strong relationships

Development of a strong relationship between the at-risk child and caregiver fosters the child's sense of self. Here are some strategies to achieve this goal.

1. Provide lots of one-to-one interactions that include touching, eye contact, hugging, cuddling, and talking.
2. Respond to the child's expressions of feelings, wants, and needs.
3. Encourage and support self-help and self-dependence in play.
4. Allow opportunities for the child to experience being an important member of the group.
5. Provide the child with a toy of his own for the day.
6. Encourage representational (symbolic) play.
7. Allow the child to often lead in adult and child play.
8. Encourage decision making.
9. Support the child in difficult tasks.
10. Allow the child to use a transitional object.
11. Use special greeting and departing rituals.
12. Encourage and praise attempts at developmental mastery.

Adapted from unpublished material developed by Marie Poulsen for workshop sponsored by University Affiliated Programs, Children's Hospital, Los Angeles, Spring 1991.

Behavior

Poor behavior organization

Certain behaviors may indicate poor organization of behavior in a child.

1. Impulsive behavior
2. Tendency to become easily overstimulated
3. Low tolerance for stress
4. Testing of limits
5. Behavioral extremes
6. Difficulty organizing his or her own play
7. Limited attention or concentration on tasks
8. Auditory processing difficulties
9. Decreased adaptive task persistence
10. Difficulty reading social cues
11. Problems in peer relationships
12. Only sporadic mastery of spatial-motor tasks
13. Inconsistent use of problem-solving strategies
14. Difficulty in handling changes in routine

Strategies for better behavior

The following strategies may help the child learn to organize and regulate his or her behavior.

1. Keep a consistent team of personnel.
2. Establish routines and rituals that allow the child to anticipate events.
3. Prepare the child for changes in activity, routines, and personnel.
4. Protect the child from overstimulation by materials, people, movement, light, and noise.
5. Provide explicit expectations and recognition of desirable behaviors.
6. Set and consistently enforce limits on harmful behaviors.
7. Match level of behavioral expectation with the level of the child's development and current capacities.
8. Help the child recover from stressful experiences.
9. Build periods of relaxation into the program.
10. Provide the child with a self-selected plan of respite when he or she is feeling overwhelmed.
11. Intervene before behavior gets out of control.

Adapted from unpublished material developed by Marie Poulsen for workshop sponsored by University Affiliated Programs, Children's Hospital, Los Angeles, Spring 1991.

Children with AIDS or HIV-positive status

Children who have AIDS or are HIV-positive present an additional set of issues for child care providers. According to the Center for Disease Control (CDC), 6,611 cases of pediatric AIDS were reported in the United States from 1981 to 1995. Children can become infected before or during birth or through breast milk from a mother who may or may not know she is infected, through sexual abuse by an infected person, or through tainted blood transfusions (under stringent control since 1985).

Not all children who test positive for HIV get AIDS, but they can be at greater risk for certain infections and opportunistic diseases. Current studies on transmission indicate that normal daily contact with a known carrier is not dangerous (Children's Hospital et al. n.d.). Nevertheless, it is important for caregivers to practice good hygiene, as detailed in Chapter 3 and Appendix A.

Due to confidentiality laws, it is entirely possible that a child care provider may not be told if a child is HIV positive. Similarly, a child may have hepatitis without an adult's awareness. Other contagious diseases can go undetected for periods of time as well; often people show no obvious symptoms when they are in the early stages of a communicable disease. Therefore, common sense dictates that caregivers use the universal protection of disposable gloves for *all* diaper changes and body-fluid cleanups for *all* children. This procedure provides protection against HIV, along with protection from other more common but potentially harmful diseases.

If a caregiver does know a child's HIV-positive status, strict confidentiality must be observed. Most states require written consent for disclosure of HIV-test results to those who have a legally justified need to know. Each center, in consultation with a lawyer, should develop policies consistent with state disclosure regulations and make clear the penalties for breach of confidentiality to third parties.

Families with a child diagnosed with AIDS or testing HIV-positive face complex psychological and social issues. Child care personnel need to be aware of the stress on parents who not only have to deal with their child's potential for serious illness or death but also a multitude of family and community issues.

3. Benefits of out-of-home care for infants with special needs

A quality infant care center or family child care home can contribute a great deal to the healthy development of many infants and young children with special needs. The more vulnerable the infants, the greater difference a nurturing and caring environment can make in their lives.

There is no question that numerous infants environmentally at risk for problems and disabilities—children who live in homes where the parent or primary caregiver is psychologically unavailable—need to be in a nurturing and responsive human environment much of the time. They need to experience adults who are responsive to them, sensitive to their cues and communications, and enjoy these interactions. High-quality out-of-home experiences, in places where adults care about young children, often compensate, at least in part, for what the infant is not getting at home. Such care may even counteract the negative experiences that some infants in nonnurturing environments are likely to have in their homes.

> In a socially and cognitively stimulating environment with emotionally available, nurturing, predictable and responsive adults, these young children would have much needed opportunities to feel good about themselves and to explore their world without fear or unreasonable restrictions. They would be able to try out a variety of behaviors in a psychologically and physically safe setting. . . . Children exposed early to such settings have the opportunity to acquire patterns of adaptation that will prepare them to cope more adequately with current and future stress and to successfully meet future challenges. (Bromwich 1985, 11)

The urgent need for quality out-of-home care also applies to infants who are both biologically and environmentally at risk, so long as the biological or medical risk can be dealt with safely in the infant care environment.

There is a great need for many of these infants to have the opportunity to experience emotionally healthy environments that foster their development in all areas. The question is, who will pay for this care if the parents cannot? In families where there is evidence of child neglect or the risk for abuse, centers that receive public funds may be asked by children's protective services to enroll such infants and young children. However, there are never enough spaces for all the infants who need quality out-of-home care.

Local organizations of infant care providers who meet for mutual support might consider advocating for children with special needs. They can solicit scholarships from civic organizations or corporations for those infants whose families cannot pay for out-of-home care.

Many infants with the needs discussed here could profit a great deal from quality infant care. There are, of course, some infants whose physicians recommend against group care for health reasons connected with medical problems (for example, severe BPD). In addition, some young children with considerable problems may need various special services provided only in certain group programs.

References

Bromwich, R.M. 1985. Vulnerable infants and risky environments. *Zero to Three* 6 (2):11.

Children's Hospital, AIDS Interfaith Council of Southern California, Affiliated Nursing School and Early Childhood Programs, & Los Angeles County AIDS Program Office. (n.d.) *Children with HIV infection* (pamphlet). Los Angeles: Authors.

Egeland, B., & M.F. Erickson. 1987. Psychologically unavailable caregiving. In *Psychological maltreatment of children and youth*, eds. M. Brassard, R. Germain, & S. Hart. New York: Pergamon.

Kirk, S.A. 1972. *Educating exceptional children*. New York: Houghton-Mifflin.

Merker, L., P. Higgins, & E. Kinnard. 1985. Assessing narcotic addiction in neonates. *Pediatric Nursing* 11 (3): 177–81.

Poulsen, M. 1991. Adapted from material developed for University Affiliated Programs, Children's Hospital workshop, Los Angeles, Spring.

Rutter, M. 1981. *Maternal deprivation reassessed*. New York: Penguin.

Tyler, R. 1990. Project TEAMS (Training, Education, and Management Skills) workshop, University of California at Los Angeles, March.

Chapter 6

Helping Children
Accept Limits—Discipline

Annabelle Godwin

The purpose of discipline is to help children learn ways of behaving that are acceptable to themselves and to others. With very young children this usually means setting limits for their safety, the safety of others, and the safety of property. Infants and toddlers need to be reassured that the people who care for them will guide and protect them.

Children often are disciplined for crying. Crying disturbs adults, but it is the way babies communicate that they need help. Crying should be neither ignored nor chastised. Comforting young children will not spoil them. Some babies cry a lot; try to comfort them and attempt to find the cause. The infant cannot tell us what is bothering her. If you have tried soothing the child for a while and the crying persists, it may be time to put the child in her crib. She might find a way to comfort herself. If she continues to cry, keep checking, holding, and trying to comfort her. You always will have to balance the needs of one child with the needs of the others in the group. It is important to check with the parent to see if anything unusual happened the night before or before the child arrived that morning. If illness is ruled out, do the best you can in the situation, but *at no time treat crying in a punitive fashion.*

Toddlers also can cry for long periods of time. As with babies, review possible causes such as teething, illness, or fear that Mommy may not come back.

Again comfort, rock, or hold the child to the extent possible in relation to the needs of other children in the group. A back rub or a cold washcloth on the child's face may help; punitive discipline will not.

A caregiver who understands child development will know that a baby's poking and pulling explorations should be allowed when they are safe. Such actions are not usually deliberate attempts to cause pain. Infants need help and guidance so that their persistent investigating does not hurt anyone or damage property. Do not use judgmental words such as *stupid* or *bad*. It is important that children feel good about themselves while learning acceptable behavior.

Firm, gentle distraction, substitution of objects that cannot hurt for those that can, or removal from the group with a clear message of what is allowed are all positive ways of responding to misbehavior. They do not demean the child. For example: "I cannot let you hit Nancy. It hurts. You may hit this pillow." Crawling infants often need protection from each other as well as help in solving problems. Explanations should be brief, such as, "Touch gently. It hurts when you pull Bobby's hair."

Accidents frequently occur because adults are often one step behind the child's developing capabilities. Infants seem to become toddlers as we watch. This means adults must be alert to the child's increasing ability to climb to forbidden places by

Do not use confinement to a playpen or crib as a means of discipline. Infants and toddlers neither understand nor respond to "time-out."

moving furniture or equipment. Watch out for equipment that tips easily. Although you may have said no, a driving curiosity pushes the toddler on to try again. Be sure valued items, dangerous substances, or objects small enough to be swallowed are out of reach. There is much less need to set limits when adults have childproofed the area.

Biting is very normal developmental behavior for toddlers, yet parents and caregivers need to unite in a firm approach: People don't bite people. Toddlers do not have the verbal ability to express their strong feelings. When they get frustrated and cannot make themselves understood, they can react primitively and bite. Parents are understandably very upset when their children are bitten, particularly if the same child is bitten repeatedly. Offer the frustrated biter something to bite on, such as a washcloth, a teething ring, or a piece of dry toast, and say, "Biting hurts people. Bite this instead." If the biter is a verbal toddler, say "Don't bite me!" or even "No! No! No!" Observe the habitual biter; take notes and see if the child reveals a pattern that illustrates what brings him to the point of biting.

There are no magic cures for this behavior. The literature offers few solutions. Experienced practitioners suggest "shadowing" the child. Assign a person to follow the toddler and intervene at each bite attempt with a stern look and a very firm "Biting is *not* okay!" Working with the parents and closely watching the child may give clues to the cause so it can be eliminated. Shadowing is possible only when there is a sufficient number of adults to do so.

When a child's behavior warrants removal from the group, some time spent with an adult might be constructive. In a center the child could sit with the director in the office and color, work on a simple puzzle, or listen to a music box. In a family child care home, the child needs extra attention from the provider. This is not a reward. It is a safety measure. The important thing is to stop the unacceptable behavior. Don't use confinement to a playpen or crib as a means of discipline; infants and toddlers neither understand nor respond to "benching" or "time-out." Hard as it might be, adults must be helpful, not punitive.

Children in the "no" stage or tantrum phase are in a growth period in which they are balancing between dependence and independence and trying to define themselves as separate people. These children need leeway, understanding, protection, guidance, and support as they seek autonomy. They are great imitators, so the behavior of adults is a major influence in toddler behavior. For example, if adults say please and thank you, toddlers will very likely add those words to their vocabulary.

Young children can become very engrossed in activities and are often reluctant to stop playing when the adult announces it is time to do so. Children

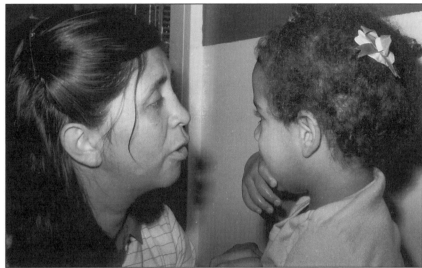

Discipline is example, simple explanation, and guidance—it is not punishment, sarcasm, or shaming.

need a warning and sometimes help with winding down their play: "It's time to put the dolly to bed. She has to take her nap, and you need to get ready for lunch. I'll help put these clothes in the drawer." People who work with toddlers should believe in children's dignity and need for respect.

Jimmy Hymes says, "Three factors conspire to make tantrums inevitable: the child's strong desires; his limited powers; [and] the fact that his feelings are still feeble and weak" (1968, 149). Adults being there with understanding and tolerance are a big plus for the child.

All behavior has a reason. To find and understand that reason, it may be valuable to ponder the following questions.

- Is the environment causing the problem?
- Do notes on the child reveal an evident pattern?
- Are adults part of the problem? In what way?
- Is it the group size? The personality mix of this group?
- Are there enough toys? Too many toys? Are they appropriate for the age range?
- At what times of the day is the misbehavior most evident?
- Is the problem behavior mainly due to a couple of children, or is it more general?
- Is there something in the children's or child's background or home life that might explain the behavior?
- Are the adults' expectations age-appropriate for the child?

People who work at centers discuss continuing behavior problems at staff meetings and with parents. Family child care providers should network with other caregivers. It is important to know when behavior is developmental and when it is out of the ordinary—not merely different. "Warm lines," free telephone services for child care providers, can offer help and guidance. Most of the time the child care provider and the parents can find solutions together. Sometimes it may be necessary to call in a consultant. Not all environments fit all children; there may be times when it is best for all concerned if the parents make other arrangements.

Most children adapt. However, it is more important for child care providers to try to meet the behavioral needs of the child who has trouble adapting than it is to make the child's behavior fit the child care setting.

Reference

Hymes, J.L., Jr. 1968. *The child under six*. Englewood Cliffs, NJ: Prentice-Hall.

Chapter 7

Helping Children Learn to Use the Toilet

Phyllis Lauritzen and JoEllen Tullis

One of the most potentially stressful topics that comes up in child care settings is when and how to help children learn to use the toilet. To avoid conflict with parents, it is a good idea to develop your own written policy on this emotional issue. Explain this policy and your philosophy to parents during the enrollment interview.

Learning to use the toilet is an important step in a child's development. In the past this process was called toilet training, and it was the adult's responsibility to train the child. Today *learning to use the toilet* (or *toilet learning)* has become a more popular description because it implies that the child participates in the learning process rather than that the adult trains the infant much as she would train a dog. The adult begins teaching when the child shows readiness to learn rather than at some magical age predetermined by the adult. The question becomes not "When should I begin toilet training?" but rather "Is this child ready to begin learning to use the toilet?"

Following this philosophy, it is important that both the parent and the caregiver watch for signs of readiness in the child. Although there is no definite age when readiness occurs, usually around age 2 the child has the muscle control to delay bodily processes until she can reach the toilet, as well as the language and intellectual maturity to understand what is expected and why.

Before a child can begin to participate actively in learning to use the toilet she should

- often stay dry for several hours;
- have fully mastered walking;
- be able to sit down and get up with ease;
- be able to communicate by sign, sound, or word the need to use the toilet;
- appear to be aware of wetting or soiling diapers, perhaps even saying that a diaper needs changing;
- perhaps exhibit such behavior as insisting on taking off a wet bathing suit or resisting the use of finger paint and gooshy clay; and
- be in a cooperative period. (Children around 2 to 3 years of age alternate between periods of negativism and cooperation. It makes sense to start toilet learning in a period when the child seems to be in an agreeable mood and open to new suggestions.)

When parent and provider agree that the time has come to begin the toilet learning process, arrange a meeting to discuss how both provider and parent can support the child in this important learning endeavor. For instance, dressing the child in clothing that is easily removed can aid both the child and the adult assisting the child. Keep in mind that learning to use the toilet, like any learning process, should be free of undue stress and presented only

Take children to the toilet frequently. Act as if you assume they will use it. If they do not, just say, "OK, you tell me later if you have to use the toilet."

when the child is developmentally ready. Some toddlers are ready much sooner than others. Watch for looks of anxiety and bewilderment. If these occur, it might be best to discontinue toilet learning until a time when the child can master it confidently.

A child may more easily master using the toilet in a child care setting where there are other children the same age to imitate. He may feel that toileting is not something being forced upon him but instead realize that it is a normal part of growing up. The child will no longer be a baby in diapers but a responsible young boy or girl who has learned an important new skill.

The following information will help centers develop policies regarding procedures for helping children learn to use the toilet. The information can be adapted for family child care homes, where there is often only one provider.

Assigning staff

It is a good practice to assign specific staff to be responsible for children learning to use the toilet. What procedures you establish will depend on the number of children ready to learn and your adult-child ratio. A caregiver may need to take his or her whole group along when a child expresses a desire to use the toilet. For this reason, it is helpful to group toilet-ready children together whenever possible. Peer example works wonders.

Some centers find it helpful to set specific times for an entire group to go to the toilet. If you use this system, keep in mind that children should not be forced to sit on the toilet. Also, remember that scheduled toilet times train staff to keep children dry—they don't necessarily help children learn to use the toilet.

Sanitation

In this age group, disease can spread rapidly through fecal-oral contact. *Careful sanitation procedures are a must.* Here are some suggestions to help keep disease down.

1. Dispose of feces, urine, and toilet paper quickly.
2. Use disposable plastic gloves or bags to avoid hand contact.
3. Place wipes and hand covers in a lined, covered waste container. Empty the container daily.
4. Keep the toileting area separate from any food preparation and eating areas.
5. Wash and disinfect seats after each use. A good disinfectant is ¼ cup bleach to 1 gallon of water (1 tablespoon per quart). Make up enough each morning for the day's use. Store this solution in

Wash and disinfect toilet seats after each use.

spray bottles by the toilet but away from children's reach. Avoid using aerosol spray around children, as lung irritation can result.

6. Have children wash their hands *thoroughly*—a project they usually enjoy very much—as soon as they are finished toileting.

7. Make sure adults wash their hands after helping each child and after cleaning toilet and potty seats.

8. Clean and sanitize adult toilets daily.

Physical setup

In a center you will need a specific area for toileting as well as defined procedures for staff. You also may need some form of potty chair. The number and type you choose will depend on the number of toilets you have and the number of children ready to learn toilet skills. There are several choices.

Seats that fit on adult toilets. Using this type of seat improves sanitation by eliminating the need to transfer waste products. However, the child needs to be able to touch the wall or a handle for support and have his feet on the ground. This may mean building platforms of sufficient size to ensure that the child will not fall or accidentally step off when using the toilet. It is also important to cover the platform with a material that is waterproof and easily cleaned. Be careful to wait until the child is off the toilet before flushing. With this arrangement, the number of children able to use the toilet at one time will be limited only by the number of toilets in your facility.

Child-size toilets. If you are building or renovating for child care, you might have child-size toilets installed. Even these, however, may be too large for some children and may need to have steps built around them.

Separate potty chairs. If you use potty seats designed to sit on the floor, you will need to develop careful sanitation procedures to ensure swift and proper disposal of waste products. Choose a style that has a removable pot. As soon as a child has used the potty chair, remove the pot and dump the waste materials into the toilet for disposal. Wipe out any remaining waste, being careful not to touch the pot with your hands. Disposable plastic gloves or bags should be used for hand protection. Deposit wipes and hand covers in a covered wastebasket.

For sanitary reasons, it is best to locate potty chairs in the bathroom. Placing them in another room is convenient for the child but increases the chance of infection because of the possibility of a child playing with the potty chair before proper sanitation has occurred. It is strongly recommended that potty chairs be placed in bathrooms next to hand-washing facilities.

Your choices and procedures need to be carefully thought through so that the child's learning to use the toilet can proceed in the proper physical and emotional environment. The adults involved—both parents and child care providers—need to have a strong commitment to working together as partners to help the child with this learning. Mastery of this important task at the child's own pace and with his or her cooperation has important implications for the child's feelings of worth and self-esteem.

For further reading

See "Bibliography," pp. 105–08.
Brazelton, T.B. 1962. Notes and comments on successful toilet training. *Pediatrics* 29 (1): 124.
Gibson, J. 1984. Time for toilet-training? *Parent's Magazine* (June): 118.
Mack, A. 1978. *Toilet learning: The picture book for children and parents.* Boston: Little, Brown.
Weissbourd, B. 1982. Toilet-training. *Parent's Magazine* (April): 92.

Chapter 8

Building Relationships with Parents

Rose Bromwich

This chapter suggests ways to facilitate supportive interactions between parents and infant/toddler care providers. How to be supportive of parents is an excellent subject for further exploration at an inservice meeting at a center or a group meeting of family child care providers.

Guidelines for interactions

1. Treat parents as partners. The parents and the provider need to work together to ensure the welfare and optimal development of the children.

2. Relate to the parents not just as parents but also as individuals with their own attributes and problems.

3. Listen carefully to what parents say about their own children, and respond with interest.

4. In informal daily contact, help parents feel good about their children and therefore about themselves by sharing with them some of the positive and fun things that happened with their children during the day. This kind of sharing helps build a positive and trusting relationship between parents and caregivers.

5. In areas of child care in which the setting is flexible, ask parents for their preferences with regard to practices with their children. If parents, however, ask the child care provider to deal with their children in a manner not acceptable in the child care setting (for example, "Don't pick up my baby when he cries"), explain why this particular practice is not allowed.

6. When problems arise that need to be discussed with the parents, discuss positive behavior as well as problems and then attempt to jointly solve the problems.

7. Parents of infants naturally are very anxious for their child and often express concerns about what may seem to the provider to be trivial issues, such as schedules and food. These demands actually reflect a deeper concern: that their child be safe, loved, and attached to *them*, the parents.

Areas of potential problems

Many young children sometimes have a difficult time leaving the child care setting to go home. This is natural and does not necessarily reflect on the quality of the relationship between parent and child. You can help minimize the parent's feeling of rejection and embarrassment by explaining that the child's reaction is quite common and natural; the child may be having a good time with his friends at that moment and not want to leave them or he may be involved in an interesting activity.

You also can encourage the child in a positive manner to make the transition from play at the child care setting to going home with the parent. For the child's sake, it is very important to support a positive relationship between parent and child.

One danger in a child care setting is that a provider's strong attachments to individual infants may interfere with his or her relationship with that child's parents. It is easy to feel "I am better for this child than her parent" or even "I care more than the parent." These are difficult feelings with which to deal. Still, child care providers must never forget that the relationship between parent and child is, in the long run, the crucial one for the child's welfare and development. A caregiver has a child for a very brief time, compared to a parent, who has her "forever."

Stresses on the parent

Many parents who bring their infants to child care settings are under some stress. Be supportive, for example, of the mother who is under stress because she would prefer to stay home with her child but cannot, or who has mixed feelings about whether to work or stay home. The mother will feel more relaxed as she becomes assured that her child is in a good, safe place, that the providers are not only her child's friends but also *her* friends, and that they care about her as a person. Parents who do not feel that the caregiver is in competition with them will not be afraid that their children will love their child care providers more than them. They will be more effective and better parents because of their supportive child care arrangements.

Infant and Toddler Care in Centers

Chapter 9

Setting Up the Environment

Linda Gordon, Ellen Khokha, Lorraine Schrag, and Ellena Weeks

Guidelines for establishing appropriate physical, psychosocial, cognitive, language, gross-motor, fine-motor, and prosocial environments for infants in child care are presented in this chapter. Note that the suggestions given are *in addition to* those required by building and safety, fire, and state licensing departments.

The well-designed physical environment invites children's exploration and manipulation.

Diapering and washing

Physical setup

1. Diapering areas should be clearly defined and accessible to facilities for washing hands, without caregivers having to touch gates, door handles, or other equipment.

2. Display a sign indicating that all staff and parents should wash hands thoroughly after each diaper change or toileting.

3. Sinks should be equipped with foot, elbow, or wrist taps so that soiled hands do not have to come in contact with the tap to turn it on and off.

4. Sinks used while diapering must be separate from those used for food preparation.

5. Dispensers for hand cream and soft, disposable towels are incentives for staff to wash hands frequently.

6. Locate all supplies for diaper changing within hand's reach of changing tables. *Never* leave children unattended on changing tables to go after supplies.

7. Provide cans with lids for soiled diapers; open cans should not be used.

8. Provide germicidal spray to clean changing tables.

9. Provide plenty of storage space for diapers and changing supplies. (Some directors find it easier to supply diapers; this eliminates the need for storage for each child's diapers and prevents diapers from becoming an issue with parents.)

10. Although miniature flush toilets are preferred, potty chairs can be used if they are emptied immediately and disinfected after *each* use, whether or not the children eliminated in them.

11. Potty chairs should never be located in the main play area.

Procedures

1. Empty the pails several times each day.

2. Use diaper wipes or disposable cloths to clean children.

(See Appendix A for a sample step-by-step diaper changing procedure.)

Although miniature flush toilets are preferred, potty chairs can be used if they are emptied immediately and disinfected after each use, whenther or not the children eliminated in them.

Food storage and preparation

Physical setup

1. Have separate food storage and preparation areas, as well as equipment for labeling each child's bottles and food jars.
2. Designate a space for recording feeding information.
3. Each classroom should have its own refrigerator and facilities for heating food so staff will not have to leave the room to prepare food.
4. Provide enough highchairs or low tables and chairs so that children do not have to wait unreasonable lengths of time before being fed. Chairs should be low enough to allow children's feet to touch the floor.

Procedures

1. Disinfect highchairs and feeding tables after each use with a solution of bleach water (¼ cup bleach to 1 gallon of water).

2. Give bottle while the child is in an adult's arms or on a pillow next to an adult; bottles should *never* be propped for an infant or carried around by a walking child.
3. An individual feeding plan should be developed by providers and parents together. The plan should be reviewed frequently to accommodate feeding changes.
4. Avoid giving infants or toddlers foods that they might choke on, such as popcorn, nuts, raw carrots, or candy.
5. Use disposable dishes, or, if regular dishes are used, use a dishwasher with a sanitization cycle or apply a sanitization rinse.
6. Daily remove food and kitchen refuse, at least to a covered container outside the center.
7. Make information available to parents about infant/toddler eating patterns, appropriate portions, and nutritional needs.

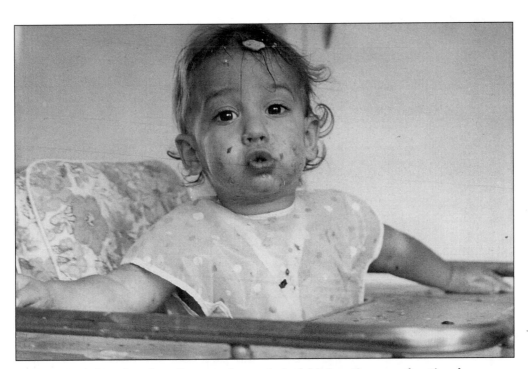

Eating time is learning time. Conversation and playful interaction are educational.

Infection control

Physical setup

1. Designate a separate shelf in the refrigerator for medication and maintain individual recording charts on dosages.

2. Provide a separate storage area for dirty linen.

3. Do laundry on site or use a service.

4. Provide a separate space for isolating a sick child.

5. Have a separate area for a staff lounge. Smoking should not be permitted where there are children, where smoke can reach the children, or anywhere that is visible to children.

6. Provide for each child a crib or cot, clearly labeled with the child's name.

7. Arrange cribs, mats, or cots to allow a walkway and work space so that staff can attend to every infant without having to step over or reach over another. This arrangement also gives easy access to and exit from the napping area.

8. Select stuffed toys and pillows that can be frequently washed and aired out.

9. All rooms should have air flowing freely, but without drafts on the floor where infants play. Good ventilation is important in building children's resistance to infection and in preventing incubation of germs.

Procedures

1. Daily wash and disinfect all toys that children use.

2. Wash linen daily.

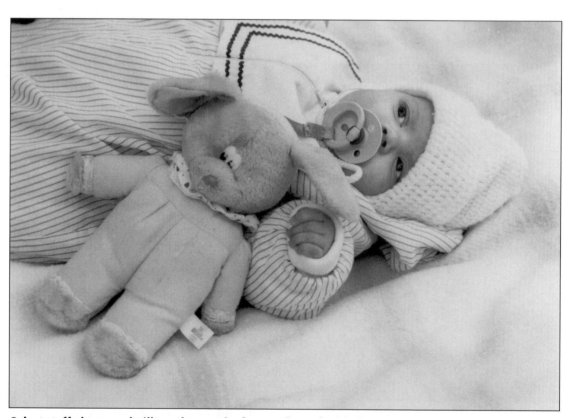

Select stuffed toys and pillows that can be frequently washed and aired out.

Safety

1. All equipment and furniture should be properly scaled and designed for infants' and toddlers' safety.

2. All equipment and play materials should be free of sharp corners, rough edges, and toxic finishes. They also should be easy to clean.

3. Storage cupboards should be out of children's reach and securely locked, especially if they contain cleaners or other toxic materials.

4. Fire escapes should be clearly identified and equipment to remove infants readily available. A wheeled crib, wagon, or laundry cart in which several infants can be placed for rapid exit should be available. A ramp also facilitates emergency evacuation.

5. Outdoor play areas should have shade to prevent overexposure to the sun and give protection from rain.

6. Play equipment should not have small objects that may be swallowed or inhaled.

7. Completely protect infants and toddlers from electrical outlets, heating grates, sewer drains, air-conditioning vents, fireplaces, stairways, and other hazards. Screens to protect hazardous areas should be constructed of sufficiently tight mesh so that objects cannot be dropped through them.

8. Install a telephone or intercom for emergency use in each classroom.

9. Carefully place and firmly secure highchairs, bookshelves, and toy shelves so that they cannot tip over.

10. The kitchen and other potentially dangerous areas should be gated to prevent access by infants. Accordian half gates are dangerous and should not be used. Solid or swing-out gates of plastic mesh work well and are safe.

Take every feasible precaution in terms of safe equipment, safe materials, and safety in every way.

11. Use only mirrors made of Mylar or shatterproof glass.

12. Keep a car seat available for emergency use.

13. Facilities should be adequately secured so that toddlers cannot leave the site.

14. Facilities should be constructed so that anyone entering the area where the children are can be seen and screened.

Psychosocial environment

1. Arrange comfortable areas where adults can sit and make themselves available for physical contact with infants and where they can position the babies to encourage infant-infant interaction.

2. Provide rocking chairs so adults can rock infants. Overstuffed chairs are comfortable for both adults and toddlers.

3. Keep carpet squares of various textures for tactile experiences as well as for children to play on.

4. Use comfortable, easily cleaned flooring material to encourage adults to sit on the floor at infant level. Carpeting should have pile low enough to allow infants to practice walking.

5. Position mirrors and other equipment at infant/toddler eye level (6 to 12 inches above the floor).

6. Arrange furniture and partitions to create areas where an individual child can get away from the whole group to be alone, with an adult, or with a small group of children. Keep all space sufficiently open for adult supervision.

7. Maintain an acoustically calm environment in which infants can attend to human voices. For example, divide spaces with furniture, use pillows to absorb sound, monitor radio and record use, and speak in calm voices.

8. Plan lighting and coloring in the rooms so they are conducive to relaxed exploration rather than overstimulation.

9. Have adequate storage space for personal belongings for both adults and children.

10. Set up an area where visitors can observe without intruding on the children's space.

11. Designate wall space at the children's eye level for displaying their work and other interesting objects. It is a good idea to cover wall space with heavy plastic so that it can be easily cleaned.

Young children learn through the leisurely handling of objects.

Cognitive environment

1. Offer equipment to climb on, crawl into, pull up on, and hold onto.

2. Have many objects that encourage experimentation and the learning of causal relationships. It is important to have toys and materials that can be used in a variety of ways.

3. Provide a variety of opportunities for tactile experiences with liquids and solids such as water, cornmeal, textured blankets, and carpet samples.

4. Display toys for all developmental levels on low shelves and tables.

5. Have designated places to get and return toys and play materials.

6. Toy boxes are useful for outside toys such as balls but are not appropriate for toys with many pieces. Infants need to have ready access to these toys; put them on shelves, not in boxes.

7. Various types of toys and materials should be stored separately so that both adults and children know which items need adult participation/supervision. This helps children develop mental classification skills.

8. Establish an environment that is primarily consistent yet allows occasional variation in toys, music, or other aspects to promote infants' interest.

9. Adults should plan and initiate activities as well as go along with children's initiations.

10. Provide safe places for children to observe adults modeling such activities as cooking, cleaning, sorting, and talking. For example, the kitchen can be behind a gate that the children can see through.

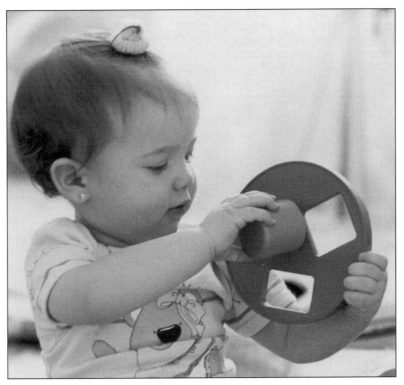

It is important to have toys and materials that can be used in a variety of ways and to allow each child time to play without interruption.

Language environment

1. Collect appropriate books for adults to share and read with infants and toddlers. Store them separately from toys.

2. Make cloth, cardboard, wooden, and nontear books available to children.

3. Make available easily read information on normal language development (for example, a chart) to make staff and parents aware of children's need for responsive adults at various stages of language development.

4. Keep record players, tape recorders, and musical instruments on site. Sing and chant with babies frequently.

5. Television is not necessary or appropriate for infants and toddlers; it tends to be misused.

Make suitable, sturdy books available to older babies and toddlers.

Gross-motor environment

1. Provide adequate indoor and outdoor space appropriately designed for infants' and toddlers' emerging needs.

2. Walkers and jumpers are not recommended for group care. Excessive weight on the feet and hips of developing children can cause misalignment.

3. Infant swings, although sometimes effective pacifiers, should not be used in lieu of physical contact with a responsive adult.

4. For older toddlers, tire swings promote social interaction. Other swings need to have safety belts and should be closely supervised to be safe for this age.

5. The environment should include a variety of surfaces such as wood, grass, sand, and plastic for tactile experiences.

6. Infants and toddlers need their own space outside or separate scheduling of space to engage safely in gross-motor activities appropriate to their developmental level, without interference from older children.

7. Have on hand enough push toys, riding toys, and simple tricycles so that children do not have to wait unduly for a turn. Several directors suggest buying at least two of each favored piece of equipment for toddlers who are not developmentally ready to understand sharing and waiting for a turn.

8. Set up ramps and bounce mattresses, as well as barrels, boxes, and other equipment to crawl in and out of.

Provide for and promote active play.

Fine-motor environment

1. The overall environment should offer ample and varied opportunities to practice and develop fine-motor abilities.

2. Keep many hand-size manipulative items readily available at the child's level. Some examples are rattles, squeeze toys, and stacking and nesting sets.

3. Have some manipulative items that require closer adult attention, such as sets with many pieces or small items like pegboards, puzzles, and small cubes, for one-to-one or one-to-two occasions.

4. Use small items also outside. Whenever possible incorporate safe natural outdoor materials such as plants, grass, sand, and wood into the program, provided babies can use and handle them safely.

5. Offer foods that can be picked up individually for the development of fine-motor skills. Some examples are noodles of different shapes, peas, small pieces of fruit, or cereals.

6. Be creative in providing manipulative equipment. Many common objects are in-

teresting to babies. Jar lids to put in and pull out of a wide-mouthed plastic container are but one example.

7. Always exercise caution. Be sure that all objects available to infants/toddlers are too large to swallow, splinter-proof, and nontoxic for mouthing.

Children need to make many choices each day. Allow them to choose among learning materials.

Social environment

Infants need to develop satisfying relationships with three distinct kinds of people in their environment: themselves, peers, and adults. Since social development is intertwined with all types of development, modifications in the environment to enhance prosocial interactions also will foster gross-motor, cognitive, and language development. The following list includes some of the equipment that infant centers have found effective in promoting positive social interactions.

Relationship to self

1. Provide baby-safe mirrors both at crawling and standing height; offer some large enough to accommodate several faces, some small enough to pick up and handle.
2. Have private space, in either a padded tunnel or a blocked-off area, where infants and toddlers can have some quiet time to themselves and yet can be easily monitored by staff.
3. Display pictures of infants at eye level.
4. Provide individual storage space at a level accessible to the toddler.

Relationship to peers

1. Make low barriers with padded risers, shelves, or equipment so that infants and toddlers can explore each other and play peekaboo without intruding in each other's space.
2. Provide low tables where toddlers can stand to play and explore messy materials with peers.
3. Have enough play materials and duplicate toys so that toddlers do not have to share before they understand the concept.
4. Provide adequate skilled adult supervision. Adults should model behavior. When toddlers interact negatively—for example, when a child bites, hits, or takes a toy away from another child—adults need to intervene appropriately.
5. Position equipment such as highchairs or strollers so that infants can engage in social interactions with others.

Perhaps the most crucial part of the environment for infants and toddlers is continuous care generously given by a small group of primary people—a parent or two, one or two caregivers, and perhaps a few other special people.

6. Protect special personal objects such as blankets or lunch boxes from being taken by other toddlers.

Relationship to adults

1. Provide adequate comfortable space so that adults can sit on the floor or at a level where infants and toddlers can reach them, thus providing a base from which infants and toddlers can explore.
2. Position changing tables and feeding chairs at a height comfortable for the adult so that caregiving routines encourage social interaction and are not tiring.
3. Foster feelings of security by using low barriers that enable toddlers engaged in play to occasionally visually check with an adult.

Chapter 10

Staffing Programs for Infants and Toddlers

Linda Gordon

Clearly establish staffing needs before doing any advertising and interviewing. Be clear about whether you are interviewing for an aide, assistant teacher, or teacher position and whether the job will be a 4-, 6-, or 8-hour daily position. Know your positions and shifts before interviewing.

Before interviewing

Have a good job description available for each position. Each job description should include the skills required, the usual duties of the position, and any other requirements that are important to you or to this position. (See sample job descriptions on pp. 69–71.)

Develop comprehensive and clear written policies. Include descriptions of general policies, benefits, holidays, grievance procedures, and staff development expectations. Your employees have the right to be informed.

Be very exact about the skills, competencies, and abilities you seek. Advertise your positions clearly. Classified ads in major newspapers often yield many responses. Advertisements at local colleges elicit fewer responses, but frequently more of the candidates have a good understanding of the field. Child care resource and referral agencies and other professional organizations maintain job banks and are good places to post your jobs.

Careful telephone screening will help you as well as the applicants. Establish that the applicant has the required experience and education. Let the person know the salary or salary scale; otherwise, time may be lost interviewing people who will not accept the salary offered. Arrange in-person interviews only with qualified, interested candidates.

Interviewing

Be available and interested when the applicant arrives for the interview. Once the candidate has filled out an application, give her or him a copy of the job description and a brochure describing your program to read while you look at the application. Now you know a bit about each other and are ready to proceed with some questions.

There are a variety of good techniques for interviewing. Those that give the candidate the most freedom in answering give you the most information about the person and her or his attitudes and philosophy. Such techniques include open-ended questions and the use of scenarios. Keep in mind that you are looking for the candidate's knowledge and feelings about infants and toddlers. Do his responses indicate a philosophy compatible with that of your program? Does she show flexibility? Do his responses reflect the education or experience claimed?

Try to sense the applicant's feelings about children and his or her philosophy of child guidance and learning.

Focus your first question on issues critical to good infant care, such as toilet learning, transitional objects (such as security blankets and teddy bears), discipline, and suitable activities and routines. Ask questions that reveal the candidate's understanding of early developmental stages and ability and interest in interacting with parents.

Here are some examples of questions.

- What do you consider the most important components of an infant center?

- What was your favorite time of the day when you worked at _____?

- Name a few activities that you consider appropriate for a 14-month-old child.

- How can a child of 10 months participate or help you when her diaper is being changed?

Here are some examples of scenarios:

- You have just set out playdough and a variety of accessories for a small group of children. They are excited and eager to begin their work. As you start to help the children take some of the playdough, one child grabs the tablecloth and pulls everything to the floor. What do you do?

- It is a very hot morning and you have decided on a water play activity with containers, buckets, and baby dolls to wash. One mother comes in late, brings her child to the group, and says, "Johnny can't play with water today. Keep his shirt and shoes on all day. I won't have him sick this weekend!" What do you do?

Avoid such questions as "Do you like children?" The answer will be yes, and you will learn nothing.

Be fair and question candidates thoroughly. If you decide at the start that someone is not right for your program, the person will sense this and be less able to respond appropriately. Sometimes people who are excellent with children are shy with adults, especially under the pressure of an interview. Look for each person's special strengths and interests. You might help an applicant relax by telling her or him a bit about your program. Participating in a conversation is often more comfortable than just answering questions. Encourage applicants to ask questions.

End interviews by letting candidates know when you will make your decision. Let them know if you will be calling them regardless of your decision. Thank candidates for coming and let them know that you enjoyed talking to them.

It usually is best not to make a job offer on the spot. Instead, review your notes and carefully consider all candidates' qualifications before making your decision.

When possible, hire for a trial period—for example, six weeks—to observe the ability of the potential employee to interact with children and to follow the program's philosophy.

Job descriptions

Sample job descriptions follow for three positions that make up the core team of an infant care program: director, teacher, and teacher assistant.

Director

Duties

When a center is small and is directed by a teacher-director, that position is defined by both the teacher and the director job descriptions.

The director is responsible for

1. All aspects of program development, supervision, budget, money management, enrollment, and facilities
2. The smooth flow of the program and its adherence to the stated philosophy
3. Overseeing the care, safety, and well-being of all children at the center
4. Staff meetings, staff training, and encouragement of continuing education
5. Enrollment, parent conferencing, parent education, and parent involvement
6. All aspects of staffing, scheduling, and supervision of personnel
7. Overall maintenance of a safe, clean, and appropriate environment
8. Compliance with codes of all state and local governing agencies: social services, fire, health departments, and others
9. Networking with the community

Supervision

1. Supervises all personnel
2. Supervised by a board of directors if the center is a nonprofit organization, by an owner if the center is owned by a nonparticipating owner, or by self if the director is the owner (in this case an advisory group is highly recommended)

Skills required

1. Thorough understanding of infant growth and development

2. Thorough understanding of appropriate programming
3. Sound knowledge of business practices
4. Ability to hire, train, and supervise adults
5. Commitment, flexibility, and good problem-solving skills
6. Ability to maintain positive relationships with infants, toddlers, staff, and parents
7. Knowledge of community resources, including health, remedial services, and child development specialists who can assess infants when there is concern about development
8. Ability to represent the program within the community
9. General knowledge of nutrition, health, and first aid
10. Ability to provide ongoing staff training sessions and to maintain appropriate materials for staff and parent use
11. Planning and evaluation skills

Experience and education

1. B.A. degree in child development or its equivalent
2. One or more courses in program administration
3. Three years' experience as a head teacher in an infant/toddler program or program for 2-year-olds
4. Preferably, some prior staff supervision experience

Additional requirements

1. Good health as confirmed by a physician's statement
2. Proof of being free of tuberculosis
3. Fingerprint clearance

Infant/toddler teacher

Duties

The infant/toddler teacher is responsible for

1. A small group of children, as their primary provider

2. The care, safety, and well-being of all children in the group

3. Planning and implementing a program geared to infants and toddlers

4. Setting up the physical environment to meet the changing needs of infants and toddlers

5. Demonstrating verbally and by role modeling a sound knowledge of good teaching practices and of child growth and development

6. Taking the place of the director in her or his absence and dealing with any special situations that may arise

7. Participating in staff meeting discussions and ongoing training regarding program, children, and parents

8. Providing information to parents about their children as well as passing on general child development information

Supervision

1. Assists in the supervision of assistants, volunteers, and visiting parents

2. Supervised by the director

Skills required

1. A good understanding of infant/toddler growth and development

2. Ability to apply this understanding of infants and toddlers to appropriate activities

3. Ability to instruct other adults, especially by good role modeling in interactions with infants and toddlers

4. Ability to work with infants warmly, calmly, and in an unhurried way

5. Ability to meet the social-emotional, physical, and developmental needs of individual infants and toddlers

6. Ability to oversee both small and large groups of children at the same time

7. Ability to maintain a safe, clean, and pleasant environment

8. Ability to plan, prepare, and present appropriate nutritious food supplements geared to individual infant/toddler needs

9. General knowledge of nutrition, health, and first aid

10. Special ability to maintain positive relationships with children, co-workers, and parents

Experience and education

1. A.A. degree in child development or its equivalent*

2. Appropriate child development courses to meet state requirements

3. Prior experience working with infants, toddlers, or 2-year-olds

4. Preferably a course in infant/toddler development and program development

Additional requirements

1. Good health as confirmed by a physician's statement

2. Proof of being free of tuberculosis

3. Fingerprint clearance

*Although the title *teacher* is used here, the minimum educational level required for this position corresponds to the entry-level Early Childhood Associate Teacher position as described in the NAEYC Position Statement on Nomenclature, Salaries, Benefits, and the Status of the Early Childhood Profession (1984).

Infant/toddler teacher assistant

Duties

The infant/toddler teacher assistant is responsible for

1. A small group of children, as their primary provider
2. The care, safety, and well-being of all children in the group
3. The physical care of children
4. Carrying out activities
5. Overseeing children's play
6. Maintaining a safe, clean, and pleasant environment
7. Demonstrating increasing understanding of child growth and development in working with children, in recording activities, and in talking with parents
8. Participation in staff meeting discussions regarding the program and activities

Supervision

1. Supervised by the teacher and the director

Skills required

1. Increasing understanding of infant/toddler growth and development
2. Ability to role-model for children, volunteers, and parents
3. Ability to apply an understanding of developmental levels to activities

4. Ability to meet the social-emotional, physical, and cognitive developmental needs of infants and toddlers
5. Comfortableness in holding and caring for babies
6. Ability to maintain a safe, clean, appropriate environment
7. General knowledge of nutrition, health, and first aid
8. Willingness to accept supervision
9. Special ability to maintain positive relationships with children, co-workers, and parents
10. Willingness to read, to learn, and to increase understanding of infant development through workshops and study

Experience and education

1. High school diploma or equivalent
2. Preferably one or more courses in child growth and development or infant/toddler growth and development
3. Prior experience working with very young children

Additional requirements

1. Good health as confirmed by a physician's statement
2. Proof of being free of tuberculosis
3. Fingerprint clearance

Staffing Schedules

The sample staffing schedule offered here can be used to staff a small program or an infant unit in a larger program. Guidelines follow (on p. 73) for its use in programs with varying numbers of children. This schedule assumes a 1:3 adult-child ratio for 12 infants. It is not recommended that group size be larger than 8, so 12 infants and 4 caregivers, despite being the correct ratio, ideally would not be all in one room.

Note: This schedule shows child care staff only. Hours for administration and housekeeping or other maintenance personnel are not included.

Schedule for 12 infants

B = paid rest break of 15 minutes
Lunch = unpaid lunch break of 30 minutes
. . . = 15-minute intervals (i.e., 8:15, 8:30, 8:45)

```
                          7:30 . . . 8 . . . 9 . . . 10 . . . 11 . . . 12 . . . 1 . . . 2 . . . 3 . . . 4 . . . 5 . . . 6
                          A.M.                                   NOON                                              P.M.

Assistant A               |————————————— B ————————— Lunch ————————|
(6 hrs; 7:30–2)

Assistant B               |————————————— B ————————— Lunch ————|
(6 hrs; 7:30–2)

Assistant C                    |———— B ————————— Lunch ———— B ————|
(8 hrs; 8:30–5)

Teacher*                           |———— B ————————— Lunch ———— B ————|
(8 hrs; 9–5:30)

Assistant D                                      |———— Lunch ———— B ————|
(6 hrs; 11:30–2)

Assistant E                                               |———— B ————|
(4 hrs; 2–6)
```

* These 8 teacher hours may be covered by more than one qualified teacher.

For 12 infants and toddlers: The teacher-director teaches the children for 4 hours a day and spends 4 hours on administrative duties. Another teacher teaches for those 4 hours.

For 24 infants and toddlers: Have two classes, each using this staffing schedule. One teacher teaches 8 hours daily. The teacher-director teaches for 2 hours and spends 6 hours doing administrative duties. A third teacher teaches for those 6 hours.

For 36 infants and toddlers: Have three classes, each using this staffing schedule. There are 3 full-time teachers. A full-time nonteaching director is needed for this size program.

These schedules are offered as a guide only. We are not recommending a group size of 12 infants and toddlers as the ideal; we feel that infants and toddlers are usually best cared for in smaller groups. We have selected this group size simply for clarity in looking at the schedule. With very little figuring, one could use half or two-thirds of the schedule to care for children in groups of 6 or 8.

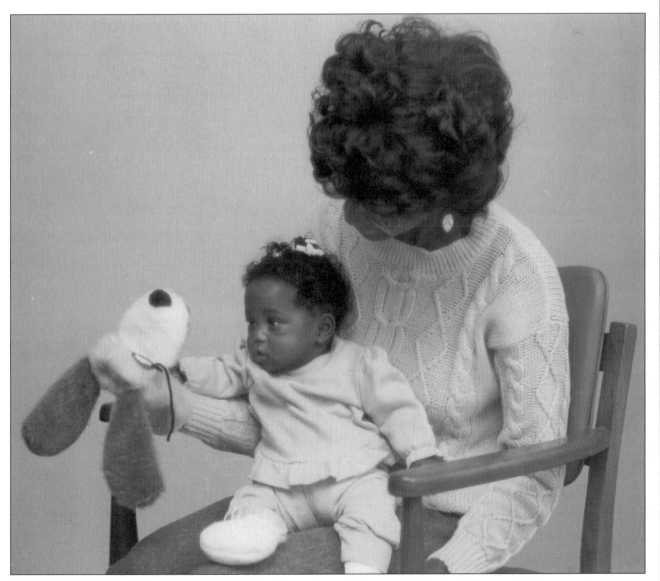

The ability to interact with infants and toddlers in an unhurried, happy way is crucial for good infant caregivers.

Sample Budget for an Infant Care Center

The following sample budget for an infant/toddler center shows the cash flow projection for a 12-month period in 1992 dollars. Allow for inflation when developing a post-1992 budget.

Income

Annual tuition ($10,560 X 24 infants)	$253,440
Registration materials fee ($25 X 24)	$600
Donations and fund raising	$5,000
Total income	**$259,040**

Expenses

Staffing expenses (74%)

Salaries	
Director/teacher	$20,000
Teachers and assistants (minimum)	$129,375
Substitutes	$10,800
Payroll-related expenses	$17,619
Staff training	$900
Professional memberships and fees	$100
Medical insurance	$16,800
Total staffing expenses	**$195,594**

Operating expenses

Food and snacks	$5,400
Art and educational materials, play equipment replacement, field trips, and professional services (music, gym, parenting classes)	$1,200
Janitorial (minimum)	$4,800
Repairs and maintenance	$1,200
Rent	$17,280
Insurance	$3,000

Utilities	$3,600
Telephone	$1,200
Publicity and fund raising	$400
Accounting and bookkeeping	$1,500
Secretarial and copying	$900
Postage and office supplies	$1,200
Equipment purchases	$1,600
Laundry	$300
Disposable diapers	$4,000
Hygienic supplies	$1,360
Total operating expenses	**$48,940**
Total expenses before contingencies	$244,534
Allowance for contingencies (3% of budget)	$7,336
Total expenses	**$259,026**
Net cash flow from operations	**$14**

Budget assumptions

- The center is open 52 weeks a year, 10.5 hours a day (7:30 A.M. to 6 P.M.)
- The center has two classrooms for 12 twelve infants and 12 toddlers.
- The director works with parents, staff, and administration for 4 hours and works in the classroom for 4 hours.
- The daily staffing schedule uses a 1:3 ratio.
- Staff salaries are moderate: teachers average $8.50 an hour; assistants $6.50 an hour; and substitutes $7.50 an hour. Staff are paid for two 15-minute breaks per 8-hour shift as required by law.
- Benefits are limited to 2 weeks' vacation, 6 paid sick days per employee, and paid legal holidays.
- Health insurance is paid at 75%.
- Payroll taxes are computed at 11%.
- Rent is calculated at $60 a month per child ($1.71 per square foot X 35 square foot per child).
- Staff education is minimal: 4 staff meetings and 2 local workshops a year.
- Two nutritious snacks are provided at 90¢ per child per day. Parents provide lunch.
- This program costs $203 per week per infant. This includes diapers and a moderately paid staff, but no cook, part-time nurse, or social worker.

For many American families, $203 per week is extremely difficult or absolutely impossible to pay for infant care, but it is a realistic cost if we are to adequately meet the needs of babies. This budget reflects moderate costs given a 1:3 adult-infant ratio, small group size, and stable staff—the factors that research indicates to be critical in providing quality care. The families who most need high-quality infant/toddler care are least able to afford it. Nonetheless, high-quality care in which staff is appropriately compensated *does* cost this much or significantly more.

How will this nation achieve high-quality child care programs that pay well enough to attract and hold trained staff yet remain affordable to families? Just as the federal government subsidizes education for children kindergarten through 12th grade, so it must subsidize—for families who want and need it—the care and education of younger children.

—Lorraine Schrag, Ellen Khokha, and Ellena Weeks

Chapter 11

Staff Satisfaction, Rights, and Status

Linda Gordon

The core of a quality program for infants is a well-trained, stable, caring staff. Much is expected of these professionals in meeting the needs of infants, toddlers, and parents. The work is exhausting and demanding. Although there is satisfaction from doing such important work well, many frustrations are involved. Salaries are frequently lower than salaries of people who work with older children. Infant care workers often report the frustration of feeling that they are at the bottom of the status ladder. Parents, insecure at leaving such young children in someone else's care, are often demanding and sharp. The combination of these frustrations may create sufficient dissatisfaction to cause staff to change positions or leave the field.

To offer quality child care programs for infants, we must retain an educated, trained, consistent staff. To do so, directors, other administrators, and boards must advocate for the rights and needs of the most important component of any influential program: the people. This must be considered a major thrust in the policy, planning, and running of infant programs.

Although the following suggestions will not fully solve the problem, they will let staff members know that they are respected and that their satisfaction is of paramount concern.

1. Work toward the improvement of salaries and benefits. Commit as much of the program's budget to salaries as possible. Scrounge for equip-

ment and supplies rather than spend money that could go to staff salaries.

2. Begin a strong campaign to educate parents and community members about the value and necessity of supporting a stable staff.

3. Encourage parents to respect and value caregivers as individuals. Parent groups can be very helpful as advocates for staff benefits and salaries. When parents are aware of how turnover affects the quality of care, they often are more willing to accept enrollment increases for improving salaries.

4. Have written personnel policies that reflect the program's commitment to staff rights. Adhere to these policies.

5. Involve staff in major decisions. This helps them understand the complexities of making the program work and gives them a feeling of ownership in and commitment to the program.

6. See to it that staff are not shortchanged on their lunch and rest breaks. This is important time for them. They will feel more relaxed and work more efficiently after a break.

7. Provide a quiet, separate place where staff can be away from their working environment—and thus, their sense of responsibility—and fully relax.

8. Provide adequate storage space for staff members' personal items.

When staff members are able to directly see the good that comes to children and parents as a result of their influence, their commitment to work is tremendously strengthened.

9. Make sure you advocate for staff in a manner that is respectful, not patronizing.

10. Provide regular staff meetings, inservice training, and continuing education so that each staff person can make contributions, feel part of a team, and continue to grow professionally and personally.

11. Provide discussion sessions in which staff members can learn good patterns of problem solving while resolving the differences that are inherent in working so closely together. Helping staff members become aware of the differences of diverse personal styles and to give and respond to clear messages can be the best investment in harmony that a program can make.

12. Take time to help staff focus on all the positive outcomes. When staff members are able to directly see the positive or the good that comes to children and parents as a result of their influence, their commitment to their work is tremendously strengthened. When staff members understand growth and development sufficiently well to become very excited by it, they are truly rewarded.

Chapter 12

Staff Meetings, Inservice Training, and Continuing Education

Annabelle Godwin

Staff meetings are vital to any early childhood center. This is where information is shared, feelings are aired, plans are formulated, and inservice training and continuing education take place. Discussions about the program should emphasize areas that the staff or director believe need improvement or reinforcement, as well as aspects of the program that are going well.

Particularly relevant subjects include hygiene (of major importance when working with infants and toddlers), working with parents, appropriate stimulation for infants and toddlers, child abuse (how to recognize and report it), the development and behavior of children in this age group, and what the staff learned at a conference. Every center has a philosophical base; discussions of the works of Ainsworth, Erikson, Piaget, and Mahler, for instance, could lead to greater understanding of the reasons behind infant/toddler behavior and the appropriate responses to it.

After the center has been open a year, it is valuable to assess which discussions were most helpful and should be repeated and which topics need to be added or handled more effectively. Some centers use a staff bulletin board for notes about various concerns to be brought up at the next staff meeting; others use a suggestion box to allow staff and parents to generate ideas and to participate in planning the staff meeting agenda. Staff meetings, inservice training, and continuing education programs should reflect the director's agenda, the staff's agenda, and the concerns of parents.

Sometimes the group may want or need to hold a staff meeting to discuss a particular child, with a good portion of the meeting devoted to looking at the child from the staff members' different points of view. The result, it is hoped, will be a further understanding of the child. Staff could suggest ways to work with him or her, or they may decide to call in an outside consultant after getting parent permission.

It is important to plan regularly scheduled staff meetings in advance so that staff members know when they are expected to be available and can make whatever arrangements are necessary. The staff should be paid for any meeting held outside of the regularly scheduled hours. It is often difficult for the whole staff to meet at once; it may be easier to have small-group meetings weekly and a full staff meeting once a month. Such an arrangement may foster openness and team spirit.

Food facilitates staff participation in meetings. For example, one center schedules a full staff meeting from 6 to 8 P.M. once a month and provides supper for those who work until 6. Other centers hold potluck suppers.

An area of growing interest that staff meetings can address is diversity. In recent years the United States

The core of a quality program for infants is a well-trained, stable, and caring staff.

Rothman and van der Zande's book, *Parent/Toddler Group* (1990), has a page and a half of common toddler phrases in four different languages: French, Spanish, Hebrew, and Farsi (see Appendix E). This is an excellent model to use for any different languages you may have in your center. A translator or a parent could help put a similar list together.

Infant/toddler care is relatively new and college courses may not be readily available locally. Because of this, staff meetings, inservice training, and continuing education are especially important to your center. Inservice training can be conducted by the director, a staff member, a parent, or an outside person knowledgeable about a certain area. The latter may cost money, but it could be money well spent. Try to plan for such occasions in your budget. Sometimes several schools can join together and split the costs. Encourage staff to attend local workshops and conferences. Pay the fees whenever possible. Visits to existing programs that you judge to be outstanding may help your staff become more knowledgeable and confident (substitutes can be used to cover such visits). Ongoing education helps staff grow professionally, and this can help reduce staff burnout and turnover, thus significantly improving the quality of your program.

In addition to a concrete plan for ongoing staff education, each infant/toddler center needs a plan for helping new employees adapt to your particular program—a plan for mentoring teachers and assistants. Most states have some educational requirements for teachers, but few, if any, have requirements for assistants. This could mean that in a group of 12 infants, one adult may have some college units and three adults may have none. If there is to be any quality in such a program, the assistants must be helped to know how to interact with the infants. They should be assisted in learning the wonders of infants and toddlers as well as their responsibilities as caregivers. A mentoring plan should begin when a new employee begins work.

Ideally, infant/toddler caregivers should recognize infant signals, plan appropriate activities, know

has become more aware of its multicultural character. No one can ignore our diversity, least of all those who live and work with children, states Gonzales-Mena (1993). She says our aim should be to promote sensitivity and problem solving as keys to providing what children need in child care. We should work to reconcile differences in ways that support a child's culture.

Sometimes parents may want the center to carry out a cultural practice they observe at home that may be inappropriate in group settings where there are children of various cultures. Such situations must be handled with sensitivity and respect.

Chang (1993) points out that working with racially mixed groups of children is a tremendous opportunity for staff to understand and appreciate diversity. Staff meetings are an ideal place to discuss these ethnic differences.

where a child is developmentally, and relate to parents with empathy and understanding. The reality is that in many cases, staff have very limited education and experience. Therefore, intensive inservice training and staff meetings are imperative for the staff both in small groups and as a whole. In California, a new Child Development Permit requires center staff to take continuing education hours annually, just as doctors and lawyers must do.

The center director is usually not only the administrator but also the mentor. She or he needs to provide the kind of leadership that encourages the staff to buy into his or her dream. The director should be able to identify weaknesses and strengths among the staff.

Role playing, discussing appropriate reading material, watching videos, and attending conferences all can help clarify the caregiver's role and the best responses in particular situations. Staff members need to be nurtured so they can feel the importance of their work and reap the pleasure of fulfillment. They need to know their opinions are valued and that they have some voice in decisionmaking. It seems apparent that, to close the gap between actual education and experience in the field and to meet the expectation of high-quality care, much guidance, leadership, and support is called for through inservice training, staff meetings, mentoring, and continuing education.

References

Chang, H. 1993. *Affirming children's roots.* San Francisco: California Tomorrow.

Gonzales-Mena, J. 1993. *Multicultural issues in child care.* Mountain View, CA: Mayfield.

Rothman, P., & I. van der Zande. 1990. *Parent/toddler group.* Los Angeles: Cedars-Sinai Medical Center Foundation.

Infant and Toddler Care
in Family Child Care Homes

Chapter **13**

Infants and Toddlers in Family Child Care

Phyllis Lauritzen

amily child care is care for a small group of children in the residence of the child care provider. It is the main source of care for infants and toddlers. Family child care licensing regulations vary with each state. If you plan to set up a family day care home for infants and toddlers, *first look into licensing regulations* by phoning your city or county social services department. In California, for example, family child care homes (referred to as family day care) are licensed by the State Department of Social Services. A family child care provider may choose from three types of family child care licenses: One adult may care for 4 infants (children younger than 2); one adult may care for 6 children younger than 12 with three younger than 2; or two adults may care for 12 children younger than 12 with four younger than 2. The latter is called a *large family child care home* and, although still in a home in a residential neighborhood, is subject to more stringent fire regulations and city regulations that vary with each city.

In family child care (with the exception of the large family child care

home), only one person cares for the children. Therefore, in the preceding chapters, which apply to infant care in general, references to administrative duties or staff responsibilities refer to the family child care provider who, being solely responsible for the child care group, is both administrator and staff—and also nutritionist, nurse, and business manager.

Family child care settings are home-like.

Fitting Family Child Care to Your Family

An integral part of family child care is the family involved in the care. Your decision to become a family child care provider affects all the members of your family. Your children and/or spouse are an important—in fact, vital—part of your program. Your family, lifestyle, and work and family schedules contribute positively or negatively to the operation of your family child care home. Be sure your own children have their personal protected spaces and areas, as well as an opportunity to participate in a positive way in the family child care operation.

The following ideas have worked well in family child care homes and are recommended by experienced providers.

1. Set hours that accommodate the family schedules—be available to child care children only after your husband and children have left for work or school and until your spouse's return from work at the end of the day. Save weekends for the family.

2. Hire an assistant for the period when your own children arrive home from school, so that neither the infants and toddlers in care nor your own children feel slighted.

3. Make sure that family members have their own areas of the home that are private and do not need to be shared or that are used only during specific times of the day, such as naptime.

4. Pay family members when they assist with the care or the work of the family child care home. This tells them how much you value their good will and hard work.

Participation from family members can add healthy human enrichment to your family child care home.

Dealing with Your Own Stress

Family child care can be very rewarding, but at times it also can be very stressful. The following tips may help prevent or relieve stress.

1. Structure some breaktime when children are entertaining themselves or napping so you can have a cup of tea or coffee and still be aware of, but not directly engaged with, the children.

2. Arrange periodically for substitute care for a holiday or part-day holiday.

3. After you've had a particularly difficult day and the children have gone home, leave the house for an evening out or schedule some quiet time alone.

4. Devise a transition time from your work day to your family time.

— Bobbie Edwards

Chapter 14

Designing the Family Child Care Environment

Jackie E. Tishler

The most important environmental factor in family child care is the provider herself—her ability to care and express her human values in her own style. Her informality and flexibility with regard to a program in her home are part of what makes family child care unique. A natural learning environment with an aware provider contributes to a loving, healthy atmosphere that fosters children's emotional and intellectual growth.

to exploring infants and toddlers; keep poisons, including medicines and cleaning supplies, locked up; put away furniture with sharp corners, especially low coffee tables, or attach rubber bumpers to the corners.

Set up play areas in corners of the living room, dining room, kitchen, or bedroom. Keep materials and toys on low shelves accessible to children. Create a quiet area, with pillows, for reading or listen-

Arrangement of the home

To make the home a learning environment requires planning. Arrange the home informally to meet the needs of young children. In addition to the areas for eating, sleeping, bathing, toileting, and diaper changing, places are needed that can accommodate crawling babies and walking toddlers. Because child care takes place in a home rather than in a center especially planned for children, childproofing the portion of the home accessible to the children is essential. Cover electrical outlets; screen off any accessible heaters or heating registers; make lamp cords inaccessible

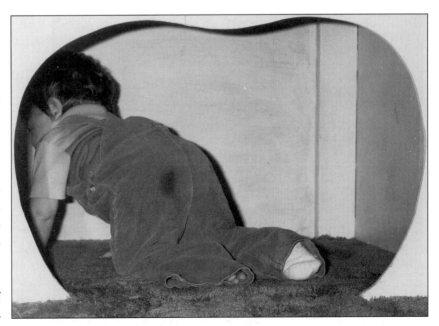

Young children need opportunities for privacy.

ing to music. Pushing a table out of the way might provide space to move to music. Because there is often a mix of ages of children in a family child care home, it helps to have a playpen to put an infant in for safety's sake when you are busy with another child and the rest of the children are actively playing nearby. The kitchen is a natural place to play with playdough, to bake bread or cookies, and to work on other similar projects under adult supervision. A fully fenced outdoor area for active play, where children have the chance to develop their large muscles, is extremely important.

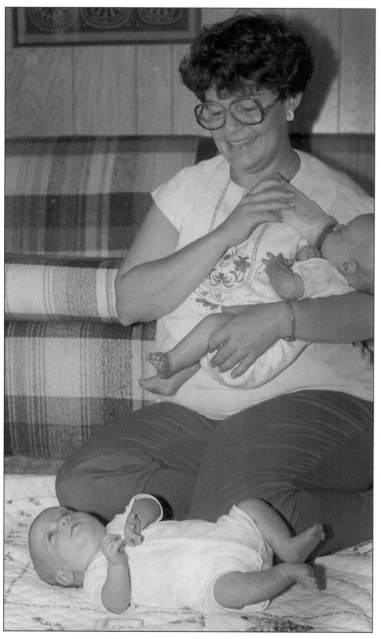

Use everyday caregiving routines as opportunities for enrichment. Chat and joke with babies.

Everyday caregiving routines

Use everyday caregiving routines as opportunities for enrichment. For example, interaction between infant and caregiver during diapering can become a natural learning experience to foster development in language, social, cognitive, motor, and sensory skills. Talk, coo, and laugh with an infant to encourage language development. Allowing the baby to kick and move without diapers promotes physical development. When the baby talks, touches, and responds to the provider, social skills are fostered. To encourage cognitive development, play peekaboo and disappear behind the diaper. Sensory skills develop as the infant feels the cold, wet diaper exchanged for a soft, dry diaper or the freedom of no clothes.

Learning can occur during everyday routines, and familiar routines can become enriching. For example, you can make cooking, setting the table, shopping, cleaning the house, making the bed, sorting laundry, fixing things, and planting a garden stimulating and fun by creating counting and matching games and encouraging cooperative efforts. Pride in accomplishment and positive self-esteem result from contributions in the family environment. Talking, laughing, singing, eating, reading, and listening to music make the home a place where children live and learn through day-to-day experiences.

The importance of play

Play for children is a way of learning. Through play children learn to express their emotions, to have fun, experiment, create, explore, and learn about themselves and other people. Through play children learn independence by trying out their ideas, learn self-confidence through achievement, and mature by using their new-found knowledge and skills. If children can satisfy their curiosity, they will enjoy learning. They love to see things happen and to make things happen.

Toys are part of play. Homemade toys and games are just as good as store-bought ones, if you make sure they are hazard free. Toys encourage children to think, to explore, and to develop skills.

Toddlers and play

As infants become active, walking toddlers, they often say no and claim that things are "mine." They like to climb and dig, move to music, touch and feel things, and bang, pull, and squeeze things. Give toddlers a variety of age-appropriate toys such as a pounding board, large beads for stringing, beanbags, a wagon and other pull or push toys, jumbo crayons and large sheets of paper, playdough, puzzles with a few large pieces, and dress-up clothes with accessories such as hats, shoes, and purses. Toddlers love to pack and unpack purses, small boxes, or any other convenient container. Also give them toy phones, dolls, cars, trucks, large cardboard building blocks, and large cartons to climb in and out of.

Small table toys help develop muscle control, sense of touch, visual skills, and eye-hand coordination. Playing at a table provides a chance for children to use their hands and to work quietly. Give children empty spools to thread on a string, zippers to zip, shoes to lace, sweaters to button, and socks to sort and match. Being able to use small muscles is an important step toward learning how to read and write.

By providing a supportive environment, you help each child grow and learn.

Learning begins at birth

Some researchers view what happens to children from infancy to 3 years of age as especially crucial to development. Warm, caring, sensitive adults help build a basic foundation for all later skills and relationships. Infants need more than food and dry diapers. They need an adult who will hold them, hug them, and smile and talk to them so they can grow and develop according to their potential.

To help infants grow and learn, give them mobiles, a cradle gym, pictures of people's faces, strips of cloth in bright colors to look at. Infants need to grasp things like squeeze toys, small balls, and hanging toys and to feel things like soft stuffed animals and blankets. They need to listen to the sounds of voices, the radio, a music box, or someone singing. As they grow, babies use their fingers to poke and bang together toys such as large safe rattles, soft toys, keys on a ring, and plastic containers. Keep in mind that any items strung together and hung from cribs or playpens could entangle an infant, so *never* leave a child unattended with such items.

Individualized learning in a mixed-age group

The home permits a family setting and an opportunity for multiage interaction. Not all children in the home will be able to do the same activity. Each child develops in his own special way. Once you get to know each child and the appropriate activities for his age group, you can guide and encourage him through the next level of development. Knowing what each child needs is the challenge of child care. By providing a supportive environment, you help each child grow and learn.

Chapter 15

Business Aspects of Setting Up a Child Care Home

Fran McHale

For many family child care providers, establishing good business procedures is the greatest challenge of their profession. Indeed, it is a crucial element for the success of any small business. Preparing a budget and setting up a bookkeeping system is possibly the most critical component of the business. Maintaining accurate income and expense records is necessary for the income-tax reporting mandated for every business. Providers also need to be skillful at conducting interviews with parents and at developing a contract that makes clear what is expected of the provider and the parent.

Estimating operating expenses to prepare a budget for a family child care business is a process as individualized as the personalities of each provider and the characteristics of each home. Obtaining budget and income information on a national level is difficult. However, through the diligent efforts of associations, training programs, and researchers, economic information has been compiled. To obtain a list of family child care associations and other sources of information, write to the National Association for Family Child Care, 1331-A Pennsylvania Ave., NW, Suite 348, Washington, DC 20004. The association in your immediate area can be of great assistance as you begin child care.

The earning potential for a family child care provider can be as high as for many jobs outside the home, except for the absence of fringe benefits for the self-employed. As with any small business, re-alizing an adequate income depends on the provider's skills in operating a business, the demand for the service, the ability of the consumer to pay the going rate, and above all, the quality of child care provided.

The first step in determining the feasibility of starting any business is evaluating your financial status to determine the amount of income you require. Once this figure is determined, the next process is researching the income potential of child care. The initial information needed to estimate income is the going rate for child care and the number of children you will be permitted to care for by your regulatory agency.

Statistics on the demand for child care in your area compared to the amount of available child care are indicators of the probability of a successful family child care business. If a child care information-and-referral service is available in your area, it can usually provide information and statistics. Information on the range of rates being charged can be obtained by contacting your local family child care association. If an association is not available, you can phone providers that advertise in the newspaper to inquire about the fees they charge. Information relative to the number of children you can care for in addition to your own children can be obtained through the office of your state's regulatory system. Be sure to inquire if any other agencies have laws with which you will need to comply.

Your potential income, before expenses, is the going rate multiplied by the number of children you will be allowed to care for under your local regulations. It is important to allow for the fact that income may fluctuate periodically because you may not always maintain the maximum number of children.

When evaluating your financial status, take into consideration that you will need to meet living expenses while going through the regulatory process. The initial startup period of advertising, interviewing parents, and enrolling children also can take considerable time.

Very few providers have families waiting to immediately use their services; for some, it can take many months to realize the maximum income they hope to earn.

Initial startup costs depend upon a number of variables. Regulatory agencies may have requirements that involve expenses ranging from a nominal fee to hundreds of dollars. Equipment and toy expenses vary depending on the amount already accumulated in the home. How elaborately a family child care home is equipped is usually the choice of the provider. Regulations are rarely specific.

Many providers find that purchasing quality second-hand equipment cuts expenses. If permissible by your regulatory agency, you can cut initial equipment costs by requiring parents to provide everything necessary for their child. Under these circumstances, the parents undoubtedly will expect your fee to be lower than that of child care homes providing equipment and toys.

Operating expenses fall into several categories. Direct expenses are the actual business expenses you incur specifically because you perform child care and are for items used solely for your business. These expenses are 100% deductible. House expenses are deductible on a percentage basis calculated with formulas developed by the IRS. These are the everyday household expenses that both your family and child care operation share. Capital expenditures are items that will last longer than one year and cost more than $100. These expenditures must be depreciated using appropriate tax laws for each category.

IRS publications 529, "Miscellaneous Deductions," and 587, "Business Use of Your Home," provide information on deductions and calculating the percentage of your home used for the business.

One category of expenses consistent across the nation is federal taxes. All small business income must be reported to the Internal Revenue Service to determine your tax responsibility, if any, for federal income-tax purposes. In addition, you must pay self-employment tax, which is your social security payment. Both the IRS and the Social Security Administration require deposits every three months to cover the taxes due on income at the time it is earned rather than at the end of the year. A tax preparer or IRS office can assist you in calculating the amount of your quarterly payments based on the income you estimate the business will earn in the current year. Failure to make appropriate quarterly payments will result in a stiff penalty if you owe a large sum of money at the end of the year. In addition, your state and local municipalities may require payment of taxes.

Self-employed persons are eligible and can make arrangements for coverage by benefits, such as workers compensation and disability insurance. Consult a knowledgeable accountant for details about family child care and options available to the self-employed.

Family child care basic expenses

Direct expenses (deduct 100%)	House expenses (deduct a percentage)	Capital expenditures (depreciate)
advertising	cleaning supplies	major appliances
bookkeeping supplies	paper goods (toilet tissue, paper towels)	equipment and toys (costing more than $100)
baby furniture		
toys and books	home repairs	furniture
craft supplies	utilities (excluding telephone)	carpets
food		home improvements
liability insurance	rent	
association dues	property taxes	
conferences		

Family Child Care Systems and Satellite Homes

Phyllis Lauritzen

Family child care homes usually are individual programs separate from other child care facilities in the community. The purpose of this chapter is to increase awareness of two administrative devices, family child care systems and satellite family child care homes. Such arrangements link homes to effect cost efficiencies and create a support base of services.

Definitions

A *family child care system* is a group of individual family child care homes banded together under an administrative umbrella. The system offers various support services that may include training opportunities, toy loans, backup personnel in case of illness or emergency, group purchasing of supplies, referral of children, help in applying for funds through the U.S. Department of Agriculture Child Care Food Program, and various health and social services for both the providers and the children in the child care homes. A family child care system combines the advantages of a small group of children in a home setting with the efficiencies possible with an administrative unit.

In contrast to a system that is a stand-alone administrative unit, *satellite family child care homes* are affiliated with a child care center and often care for infants and toddlers until they become eligible to enter the center at age 2 or whatever age is deemed appropriate. The center is used for train-

ing purposes and provides support services similar to those provided by family child care systems.

Advantages and disadvantages of systems and satellite homes

For the sponsoring agency

There are potential advantages and possible disadvantages to family child care systems and satellite family child care homes. For the sponsoring agency, the start-up costs are low. No space is needed for the provision of the child care—it is provided in the private home of the family child care worker. Space does need to be provided, however, for the administrative unit.

A family child care system is flexible in that the number of homes used can be adjusted to the number of infants and toddlers requiring care, whereas an infant center has a predetermined capacity for a set number of children. If the sponsor is an employer and if quality care is provided, benefits may include increased ability to recruit employees and less turnover and absenteeism.

Possible disadvantages for the sponsors include the difficulty of recruiting either new or licensed family child care providers and maintaining quality controls if the family child care providers have independent contractor status (see Chapter 10 for a more complete discussion of this issue).

For the family child care provider

Potential advantages and disadvantages also exist for the family child care provider. The family child care provider is often the only person caring for the children, since care is offered in a private home. The resulting isolation and the complete responsibility for the group can be overwhelming at times. Being part of a system means the provider could phone a resource person at the system office for support and help. It means the availability of a variety of services such as reduced cost of materials, assistance with record keeping, and access to training and toy loans. Providers may also receive training to further their professional development.

The provision of backup personnel in case of the provider's own illness or emergencies can be particularly helpful. Family child care providers have difficulty taking a day off for illness because backup help is not available and parents cannot always take time off from work. Being part of a system provides sick leave for the provider and more stability of care for the parent.

Another benefit for the provider is the prestige of being part of a respected child care system. Family child care providers are sometimes unjustly referred to as "just babysitters." A member of a system could say, "I work for XYZ Child Care," which sounds more professional.

A possible disadvantage to the family child care provider is the loss of independence. Family child care providers may like being their own bosses. Being part of a system or being a satellite family child care home entails certain obligations and the possibility of administrative personnel becoming involved in the operation.

The quality of the personnel of the administrative unit is crucial. Working with the child care providers, respecting their abilities, and being responsive to their concerns promotes a productive and cost-effective relationship.

The first step to implementation of a system: A feasibility study

If you are considering setting up a family child care system or adding satellite family child care homes, the first step is to obtain information on different program models developed nationally (see the references at the end of this section) and then research the child care conditions and resources in the local community. The number of family child care homes and the average cost of care in an area may be obtained from the local resource and referral agency if one exists (contact the National Association of Child Care Resource and Referral Agencies for regional listings) and will help determine budgets and the number of new homes that may need to be recruited.

Familiarity with state regulations for family child care homes, which vary from state to state and run the gamut from mandated licensing to registration to no regulations whatsoever, is a required piece of information. A survey of parents to determine their child care needs and preferences is an important determining factor in whether to proceed with the implementation of a system or satellite homes.

A projected budget is the next step in the feasibility study. The size of your budget will be determined by the configuration of your system, which may vary from a few homes to an extensive network. (A sample budget for an extensive family child care network in Los Angeles is included in Chapter 10 as an example of one program model.)

Given the right conditions, systems or satellite homes can provide a viable, flexible, cost-effective supplement or alternative to infant and toddler care in centers. They provide more choices for parents seeking quality child care as well as the opportunity to match infant/toddler settings with the infant care needs of children and parents. They also provide more options for child care providers, some of whom prefer to work independently in their homes as care providers, and some of whom, although working in their homes, would appreciate being part of an administrative system that provides cost efficiencies and support services.

The following organizations and agencies are sources of information on family child care systems.

- California Department of Education, Child Development Division, 721 Capitol Mall, Sacramento, CA 94244-2270; 1-800-445-7216.

    The California Department of Education contracts with 24 family day care systems throughout the state of California, including

Many parents prefer the more home-style atmosphere of family child care settings for their infants and toddlers. Family child care systems and satellite family child care homes provide the administrative structure that permits cost efficiencies and services.

5 sponsored by public education agencies and 19 sponsored by provate agencies, to provide subsidized child care for income-eligible children in family child care homes.

- Child Care, Inc., Neighborhood Child Care Initiatives Project, 275 Seventh Avenue, New York, NY 10001; 212-929-7604.

  Cynthia Rowe, director of the Neighborhood Child Care Initiatives Project, has written a comprehensive how-to guide, *Developing and Managing a Family Day Care Network* (1989).

- The Children's Foundation, 725 15th St., NW, Suite 505, Washington, DC 20005; 202-347-3300.

  The foundation supplies information and materials on home-based child care issues and sponsors a resource clearinghouse.

- Council for Early Childhood Professional Recognition, 1718 Connecticut Ave., NW, Suite 500, Washington, DC 20009; 1-800-424-4310.

  The council administers the Child Development Associate National Credentialing Program for family child care providers.

- National Association for Family Child Care, 1331-A Pennsylvania Ave., NW, #348, Washington, DC 20004; 1-800-359-3817.

  A membership organization for family and group child care providers, advocates, parents, and support personnel, NAFCC offers accreditation for family and group providers. It also publishes a quarterly newsletter and offers insurance information.

- National Association of Child Care Resource and Referral Agencies, 1319 F Street, NW, Suite 606, Washington, DC 20004-1106; 202-393-5501.

  This organization maintains a list of child care resource and referral agencies throughout the country.

- National Council of Jewish Women, Inc., 53 West 23rd Street, New York, NY 10010; 212-645-4048.

  A publication by the council, *Employers and Family Day Care* (1991), provides up-to-date information on employer-sponsored systems across the country.

- Virginia State Division of Licensing, 8007 Discovery Drive, Richmond, VA 23288; 804-473-2100.

The state of Virginia (which has no mandatory licensing of family child care homes) licenses family child care systems, which in turn certify participating homes. To obtain licensing regulations for systems, contact the Licensing Division.

- Windflower Enterprises, 142 Claremont St., Colorado Springs, CO 80910.

  This is a provider-oriented organization that specializes in training and technical assistance.

Managing family child care systems and satellites

To establish and maintain effective systems of family child care homes or satellite-center linkages requires administration beyond that required for individual homes. To begin with, determining whether providers in satellite homes or in independent family child care systems should be employees or independent contractors is an administrative decision that influences the recruitment of providers and the sponsor's cost and supervisory control.

Differences in the status of providers

Independent contractor status. The sponsor contracts with the family child care home to provide child care services. Sponsoring agencies may suggest training and/or activities for children but may not require attendance at training sessions or supervise family child care providers directly.

Independent contractors—i.e., the family child care home providers—may hire assistants and delegate work as they desire. Hours of work are determined by the needs of the parents served and not by the sponsoring agency. Providers are free to enroll children from other families and are not required to serve only the sponsoring agency's families.

Child care is provided at the contractor's site, and contractors furnish their own supplies and usually provide their own insurance coverage. The agreement between the contractor and the sponsoring agency clearly states the provisions of the arrangement, including reasons for termination by either party. New agreements are signed periodically (agreements usually are reviewed once a year). In-

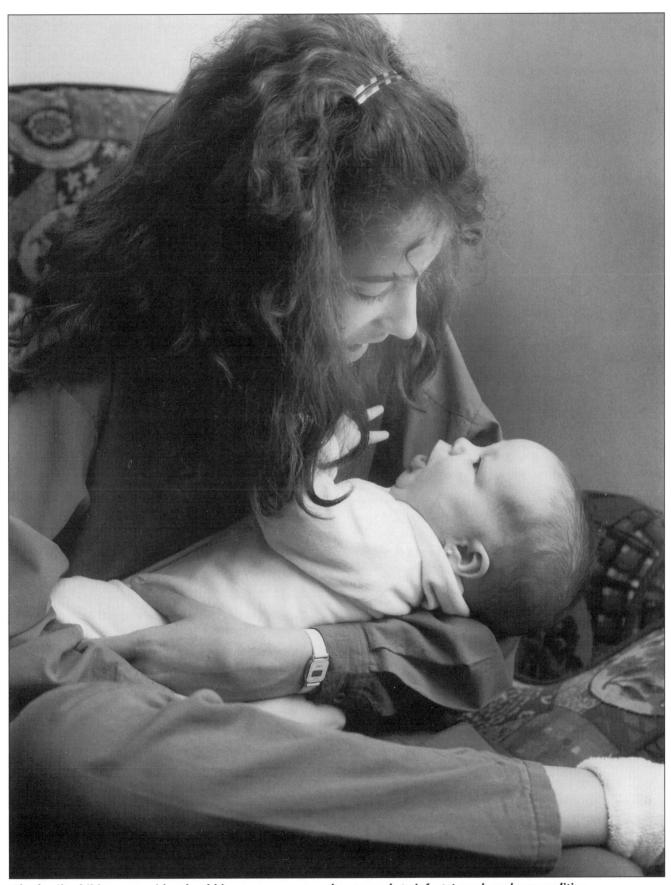

The family child care provider should be a warm person who responds to infants' needs and personalities.

Chapter 16: Family Child Care Systems and Satellite Homes

dependent contractors are paid by the job, not by the hour.

Employer-employee status. Family child care providers are employees and are paid a wage. The sponsor is an employer responsible for tax deductions, benefits, and so on.

Employers have the right to supervise, mandate training, and fix the hours and location of the child care. Employers are liable for the quality of the child care provided. They also may limit enrollment of children in the family child care homes to a specified group of parents.

Job descriptions and sample budget

Below and on the next page are job descriptions for the coordinator of a family child care system, an assistant coordinator, and the child care provider. The standards regarding the skills, experience, and education requirements for persons employed by family child care systems and satellite family child care homes are suggested minimum requirements and are not mandated by any licensing agency.

The sample budget for a family child care system appearing on pp. 100–101 will be of use to anyone thinking about setting up such an operation.

Family child care system coordinator

Duties

The coordinator is an employee of the system. She or he

1. Recruits family child care homes
2. Clarifies (under the direction of the sponsor) the status of the family child care provider as either an independent contractor or an employee
3. Assists and counsels parents seeking child care within the system (the choice of a particular home from among those available is the decision of the parent)
4. Maintains records of child placement and attendance and the financial records necessary for budget purposes
5. Provides support services to family child care providers
6. Makes referrals to community agencies as required
7. Oversees the smooth functioning of all aspects of the program

Skills required

1. Thorough understanding of child growth and development from infancy through age 12
2. Understanding of age-appropriate activities
3. Knowledge of sound business practices
4. Knowledge of and respect for the unique features of family child care
5. Ability to build strong positive relationships with employers, parents, and family child care providers
6. Knowledge of community resources

Experience and education

1. A.A. degree in early childhood education or its equivalent
2. One or more courses in business or program administration
3. At least one year of experience as a family child care provider

Assistant coordinator

Duties

The assistant coordinator (if the size of the program warrants this position) is also an employee of the system. He or she

1. Implements the support services provided for family child care homes
2. Keeps records as required by the system coordinator
3. Recruits new homes as needed
4. Substitutes for the system coordinator as needed

Skills required

1. Knowledge of child growth and development from infancy through age 12
2. Understanding of age-appropriate activities and environments
3. Knowledge of and respect for unique features of family child care
4. Ability to establish positive relationships with children, parents, family child care providers, and administrators
5. Knowledge of community resources

Experience and education

1. Some course work in child development or early childhood education
2. At least one year of experience as a family child care provider

Family child care provider

Duties

The family child care provider is licensed by the appropriate agency to provide child care in her or his home. The provider may be an employee of the system or operate as an independent contractor (see the discussion at the beginning of this chapter). He or she

1. Supervises the care, safety, and feeding of a small group of children in the home
2. Provides an environment that is safe and contains activities appropriate for the age of the children in the group
3. Works cooperatively with parents for the benefit of the children
4. Works cooperatively with the administration of the system
5. Maintains the records necessary for the operation of a small child care business

Skills required

1. Understanding of child growth and development from infancy through age 12
2. Knowledge of age-appropriate activities
3. Understanding of sound business procedures
4. Knowledge of nutrition, health, and first aid
5. Warm personality and willingness to respond to infants' needs in a manner that fosters emotional growth and development
6. Ability to work with children, parents, and system employees

Experience and education

1. Some courses in early childhood education or child development preferred
2. First aid course desirable
3. Previous experience working with children as a parent, in a child care setting, or as a family child care provider
4. Experience working with adults in groups

Sample Budget for a
Family Child Care System

The following sample budget for a family child care system shows the cash flow projection for a 12-month period in 1988 dollars. Allow for inflation when developing your budget. (Compare this budget with the budget for an infant care center, pp. 74–75.)

Income

Annual tuition ($4,940 x 24 infants)	$118,560
Registration materials fee ($25 x 24 infants)	$600
Total income	$119,160

Expenses

Staffing expenses (86%)

Family child care coordinator's salary	$18,000
Payroll-related expenses	$1,980
Training expenses for providers	$500
Professional memberships	$100
Reimbursement for family child care providers (per child: $65 per week or $3,380 per year x 24)	$81,120
Total staffing expenses	$101,700

Operating expenses (11%)

Janitorial	$1,200
Office rent	$3,694
Utilities	$1,200
Telephone	$1,200
Publicity and fundraising	$400
Accounting and bookkeeping	$1,500
Secretarial and copying	$900
Postage and office supplies	$1,200
Equipment purchases	$1,600
Allowance for speakers for parent educaton meetings	$100
Total operating expenses	$12,994

Total expenses before contingencies	$114,694
Allowance for contingencies (3% of budget)	$3,441
Total expenses	$118,135
Net cash flow from operations	$1,025

Budget assumptions

- Office rent is based on the rental of 12' x 15' office at $1.71 per square foot.

- The family child care providers are independent contractors.

- The family child care provider is responsible for arranging and paying for substitutes (although the system could provide the names of possible subs).

- Meals, snacks, art and educational materials, replacement of play equipment, repairs and maintenance, insurance, laundry, diapers, and hygiene supplies included in the budget for an infant care center are eliminated because they are provided by the family child care provider, not by the system.

- A budget item of $1,600 for equipment purchase covers a toy loan program available to family child care providers.

- Classroom space is not budgeted because care is provided in the home as part of the contract.

- Janitorial services and utilities are reduced by two-thirds because space requirements are smaller than those of a center, consisting of space only for administration, not for child care.

This program costs $95 per week per infant, compared with the infant center cost in this book of $203 per week. If satellite family child care homes attached to a child care center are used, some of the administrative costs for space and personnel and some office expenses might be spread over the total operation. This would further reduce the expenses shown on this budget, which is for a stand-alone family child care system.

The number of family child care homes in a system or satellite family child care homes connected with a center depends upon the number of children placed in each home. The number of children placed in each home depends upon the state licensing regulations regarding the number of infant/toddlers that can be cared for in each family child care home, the type of family child care license the provider has, and the type of contract the family child care homes and the sponsoring agency have (see discussion on pp. 96, 98 of independent contractor vs. employer/employee status).

For example, California issues licenses to homes to care for four infants. Hence only six homes caring for four infants each would be needed to care for 24 infants/toddlers if the family child care homes were employees and the system used all the child care spaces each home had available. If the system and the homes had an independent contractor arrangement, the family child care provider may not care exclusively for children referred by the system. If only three system children out of a licensed capacity of four are cared for in each home, the system needs eight homes to care for 24 children. If the home caregivers care for mixed ages (that is, three children younger than 2 years of age and three older than 2) and if the sponsoring agency contracts with the family child care providers as independent contractors, the agency could contract for all three spaces available for infants/toddlers. This would still leave three spaces for older children that the family child care provider could fill with nonsystem children. This arrangement again would require a minimum number of eight homes but would mean more income for the provider, who would be caring for six children as opposed to four under an infant care license and independent contractor status.

A family child care provider as an independent contractor operating at capacity and caring for six children at $65 per child per week has a possible gross income of $20,280 annually. In addition, by using her home as a place of business she has the benefit of tax deductions, such as a portion of the rent or house payment, a portion of utilities, and child care related repairs and maintenance. Also, a portion of any home improvements in the area used by the children is tax deductible. This reimbursement compares favorably with the infant center teacher's salary of $8.50 per hour or $17,000 per year. However, a family child care provider who has children of her own would not be able to care for six other children because the license capacity includes the family child care provider's own children. Therefore, $3,380 would need to be deducted from the possible gross income of $20,280 for each of the provider's own children younger than 12 who is present during child care hours.

Finding Help in Your Community

Annabelle Godwin

Because there occasionally will be times when child care providers need outside help, directors and family child care workers should be aware of the resources in their community.

A child care resource-and-referral agency (R&R) serves the specific needs and interests of its particular community. These agencies (also called information-and-referral agencies) are usually community-based and nonprofit. Their main function is referring parents to a child care program that is best suited to a child's needs. Many also offer toy loans, libraries, parent support services, and technical assistance to providers.

INFO is an information-and-referral service supported by United Way and other agencies in many cities throughout the country. The phone line specialists are on duty around the clock. They deal with a wide range of situations such as family problems, health needs, transportation, and legal help. Some communities have family service agencies sponsored by religious groups. Some towns may have a community-coordinated child care council or a child guidance clinic that deals with behavior problems. There may be agencies that have a "warm line" for parents or child care people to call for help concerning a particular kind of behavior.

If few such resources exist in your area, try forming a support group of people interested in or working with infants and toddlers. Employers, child care providers, members of the health professions, parents, social workers, educators, and psychologists are all possible members of such a group. The group would set its own agenda regarding what it wants to do for the community to better the lives of the very young and their parents.

Some infant/toddler directors have expressed a desire for increased focus on infants and toddlers at local, state, and national conferences. One AEYC chapter sponsored a well-attended conference solely on infant/toddler issues. A community college and R&R collaborates on infant/toddler rap sessions for directors and lead teachers. Participants often choose the topics. Sometimes an expert is invited to join the group. These directors are looking for opportunities to share what they have learned and to discuss situations about which they want to know more.

This area of child care is an ever-growing field. More than 50% of the calls in our R&R come from parents seeking infant and toddler care. (California has more than 1,100 infant/toddler programs.)

The Infant Task Force that put this book together became more than a committee formed to produce written materials. We all learned from each other and wanted to extend our association, so we continued to meet to discuss new books in the field. We became and are a support network for each other. We monitor, support, and even initiate legislation. We are vigilant to maintain and upgrade standards in the child care field.

Others can take on similar tasks in their communities. In this way, we all can better protect our nation's youngest and most vulnerable children.

Bibliography

Much literature is available on infants and toddlers. Some of it is excellent; some of it is not. We suggest you be wary of too much emphasis on regimentation in dealing with very young children and also of the push of early academics and reading. This list represents what we think is the best thinking on infant/toddler care.

Infant and toddler development

Brazelton, T.B. 1974. *Toddlers and parents: A declaration of independence.* New York: Delacorte. Deals with negativism and separation during the toddler stage as well as various situations in today's world such as the single parent and working mothers.

Brazelton, T.B. 1983. *Infants and mothers: Differences in development,* 2d ed. New York: Delacorte. Interesting treatment of different ways babies develop in the first year of life. Descriptive, informative, with practical suggestions.

Carew, J.V., I. Chan, & C. Halfar. 1976. *Observing intelligence in young children.* Englewood Cliffs, NJ: Prentice-Hall. Striking differences in children's intellectual development led the authors to suggest 14 ways that mothers can facilitate growth in 1- to 3-year-olds.

Caruso, D.A. 1988. Research in review. Play and learning in infancy: Research and implications. *Young Children* 43 (6): 63–70.

Chess, S., Thomas, A., & H.G. Birch. 1978. *Your child is a person.* New York: Penguin. Written for parents and based on a famous study that followed children for 20 years to document their different temperamental types and how their development and other people's reaction to them were affected.

Daniel, J.E. 1993. Infants to toddlers: Qualities of effective transitions. *Young Children* 48 (6): 16–21.

Dombro, A., & L. Wallach. 1988. *Ordinary is extraordinary.* New York: Simon & Schuster.

Dunn, J. 1977. *Distress and comfort.* The Developing Child Series. Cambridge, MA: Harvard University Press. Examines theories and research for explanations of the sources of infant distress cries and how variations of early interactions may affect the baby's ability to obtain comfort.

Evans, J., & E. Ilfeld. 1981. *Good beginnings.* Ypsilanti, MI: High/Scope. Easy-to-read book stresses the role of parents as the newborn child's most important teacher.

Furman, E. 1992. *Toddlers and their mothers.* Madison, CT: International Universities Press.

Gonzalez-Mena, J. 1986. Toddlers: What to expect. *Young Children* 42 (1): 47–51.

Greenberg, P. 1991. *Character development: Encouraging self-esteem & self-discipline in infants, toddlers, & two-year-olds.* Washington, DC: NAEYC. Twelve essays, with practical, problem-solving points of view, for reflective teachers, directors, and students who care about developing good people while working with very young children.

Greenspan, S.I., & N.T. Greenspan. 1985. *First feelings: Milestones in the emotional development of your baby and child.* New York: Penguin.

Honig, A.S. 1985. The art of talking to a baby. *Working Mother* (March): 72–78.

Honig, A.S. 1988. Research in review. Humor development in young children. *Young Children* 43 (4): 60–73.

Honig, A.S. 1989. Quality infant/toddler caregiving: Are there magic recipes? *Young Children* 44 (4): 4–10.

Honig, A.S. 1993. Mental health for babies: What do theory and research tell us? *Young Children* 48 (3): 69–76.

Hughes, F.P., J. Elicker, & L.C. Veen. 1995. A program of play for infants and their caregivers. *Young Children* 50 (2): 52–58.

Lally, J., A. Griffin, E. Fenichel, M. Segal, E. Szanton, & B. Weissbourd. 1995. *Caring for infants and toddlers in groups: Developmentally appropriate practice.* Washington, DC: Zero to Three/National Center for Clinical Infant Programs. Hands-on guide demonstrates how to build strong relationships—between children and their families, between families and caregivers, among children, and among adults—in the child care setting. Includes illustrations of appropriate and inappropriate practice, developmental milestones for babies and toddlers, and resources for further learning.

Leach, P. 1981. *Your baby and child: From birth to age 5.* New York: Knopf. Written for parents, with chapters on birth, the newborn through preschool-age child, first aid, and playthings for children of different ages; includes growth charts and 650 illustrations. By the same author: *Babyhood.*

McCall, R.B. 1979. *Infants.* Cambridge, MA: Harvard University Press. Readable review of recent research on infants.

Richards, M. 1980. *Infancy.* New York: Harper & Row. Comprehensive survey of first year. Authoritative but easy-to-read and well-organized, with many photographs, good bibliography, and index.

Sroufe, F. 1977. *Knowing and enjoying your baby.* Englewood Cliffs, NJ: Prentice-Hall. Describes the growth of smiling, laughter, joy, fear of the unfamiliar, and other emotions so that a sensitive caregiver can learn to be responsive to a baby's signals.

Weissbourd, B., & J. Musick, eds. 1981. *Infants: Their social environments.* Washington, DC: NAEYC. Includes chapters by 12 different authors on such subjects as infant research, appropriate curriculum, public policy, and supporting parents.

Wittmer, D.S., & A.S. Honig. 1994. Encouraging positive social development in young children. *Young Children* 49 (5): 4–12.

Starting an infant/toddler center

Balaban, N. 1992. The role of the child care professional in caring for infants, toddlers, and their families. *Young Children* 47 (5): 66–71.

Bergstrom, J.M., & J. Shoemaker. 1983. Guidelines for expanding your program to serve infants and toddlers. *Child Care Information Exchange* (November): 17–19.

Bronson, M. 1995. *The right stuff for children birth to 8: Selecting play materials to support development.* Washington, DC: NAEYC. A user-friendly handbook that describes play materials beneficial to children from birth to age 8, featuring clear explanations of what children are like at each age and concrete information on what they enjoy doing.

Cataldo, C. 1982. *Infant and toddler programs: A guide to very early childhood education.* Reading, MA: Addison-Wesley. Comprehensive text on everything to know about starting infant and toddler programs.

Frost, J., ed. 1977. *Developing programs for infants and toddlers.* Washington, DC: Association for Childhood Education International. Series of papers presented at a conference on infancy, including an excellent article describing the characteristics of poor versus good programs for infants and a well-designed chart on planning environments using Piagetian concepts geared to age levels.

Green, M.I. 1977. *A sigh of relief.* New York: Bantam. The definitive book of first aid and health care; well-indexed, easily understood suggestions with diagrams.

Honig, A.S. 1985. High quality infant/toddler care: Issues and dilemmas. *Young Children* 41 (1): 40–46.

Honig, A.S., & R.J. Lally. 1981. *Infant caregiving: A design for training.* Syracuse, NY: Syracuse University Press. A must for any infant program, with chapters on infant development and inservice training of infant caregivers.

Kendall, E.D. 1983. Research in review. Child care and disease: What is the link? *Young Children* 38 (5): 68–77.

Lurie, R., & R. Neugebauer. 1982. *Caring for infants and toddlers,* Vols. 1–2. Redmond, WA: Child Care Information Exchange. Articles from the *Child Care Information Exchange* magazine selected for their relevance to caring for infants and toddlers.

Mack, A. 1978. *Toilet learning: The picture book technique for children and parents.* Boston: Little, Brown. A book on toilet learning, as opposed to toilet training, that explains the philosophy both to parents or staff; includes an entertaining story to read to a toddler ready for toilet learning.

McCracken, J., ed. 1984. *Administering programs for young children.* Washington, DC: NAEYC.

Robertson, A., & B. Overstad. 1979. *Infant-toddler growth and development: A guide for training child care workers.* St. Paul, MN: Toys 'n Things Press, Resources for Child Caring. Provides child care workers with a better understanding of normal development, appropriate toys and activities, and physically and emotionally safe environments.

Weisner, M.S. 1982. *Group care and education of infants and toddlers.* St. Louis, MO: Mosby. Well-written and well-indexed text on group care for infants and toddlers.

Starting a family child care home

Auerbach, S., ed. 1978. *Creative centers and home.* New York: Human Sciences Press. Explains infant care, planning and developing family child care, and approaches to designing and creating the child's environment.

Baker, A.C. 1992. A puzzle, a picnic, and a vision: Family day care at its best. *Young Children* 47 (5): 36–38.

Bronson, M. 1995. *The right stuff for children birth to 8: Selecting play materials to support development.* Washington, DC: NAEYC. A user-friendly handbook that describes play materials beneficial to children from birth to age 8, featuring clear explanations of what children are like at each age and concrete information on what they enjoy doing.

Calendar Keeper, rev. ed. 1978. St. Paul, MN: Toys 'n Things Press, Resources for Child Caring. A family child care record-keeping system, including forms and activities for children.

Colbert, J., ed. 1980. *Home day care: A perspective.* Chicago: College of Education, Roosevelt University. Collected articles on family child care, including research and examples of model training programs.

Collins, A., & E. Watson. 1976. *Family day care*. Boston: Beacon. Includes chapters on family child care and cooperative child care exchange and information-and-referral agencies as a bridge to family child care homes and family child care associations.

Corsini, D.A., S. Wisensale, & G-A. Caruso. 1988. Family day care: System issues and regulatory models. *Young Children* 43 (6): 17–23.

DeBord, K. 1993. A little respect and eight more hours in the day: Family child care providers have special needs. *Young Children* 48 (4): 21–26.

Deyampert, E. 1992. Family day care: What keeps parents coming? *Young Children* 47 (4): 60.

Fosberg, S. 1981. *Family day care in the United States: Summary of findings, Vol. 1*. Washington, DC: U.S. Department of Health and Human Services, Head Start Bureau. Abt Associates report of the National Day Care Homes Study of family child care in Los Angeles, Philadelphia, and San Antonio; includes statistics on children in care, caregivers, and fees, plus recommendations.

Galinsky, E., C. Howes, S. Kontos, & M. Shinn. 1994. Public policy report. The study of children in family child care and relative care—Key findings and policy recommendations. *Young Children* 50 (1): 58–61.

Garcia, R. 1985. *Home centered child care: Designing a family day care program*. San Francisco: Children's Council of San Francisco. Covers environment design, infant/toddler development, value of play, and standards for quality care.

Gonzalez-Mena, J. 1991. *Tips and tidbits: A book for family day care providers*. Washington, DC: NAEYC.

Greenberg, P. 1987. Ideas that work with young children. What is curriculum for infants in family day care (or elsewhere)? *Young Children* 42 (5): 58–62.

Kontos, S. 1992. *Family day care: Out of the shadows and into the limelight*. Washington, DC: NAEYC.

Manfredi-Petitt, L.A. 1991. Ten steps to organizing the flow of your family day care day. *Young Children* 46 (3): 14–16.

McClain, D., & P. Lauritzen. 1981. *Infant family day care training*. San Fernando, CA: Mission College. Consists of program manual, discussion and workshop sheets, and final report of a project funded by the Women's Equity Act for the training of infant family care providers.

Modigliani, K., M. Reiff, & S. Jones. 1987. *Opening your door to children: How to start a family day care program*. Washington, DC: NAEYC. A readable book covering everything about starting a family child care program.

Sale, J., & Y. Torres. 1979. *I'm not just a babysitter*. Pasadena, CA: Pacific Oaks College. Classic study and project funded by the Children's Bureau, Office of Child Development, U.S. Department of Health, Education and Welfare, that raised consciousness on family child care as a child care alternative.

Seefeldt, C., &S L. Dittman, eds. 1975. *Family day care*. Washington, DC: U.S. Government Printing Office.

Shuster, C.K., M. Finn-Stevenson, & P. Ward. 1992. Family day care support systems: An emerging infrastructure. *Young Children* 47 (5): 29–35.

Sigovich, D.A. 1994. Viewpoint. Positive regulating of family child care providers. *Young Children* 49 (5): 80–81.

Squibb, B. 1980. *Family day care: How to provide it in your home*. Cambridge, MA: Harvard Common Press. Subjects include licensing, the home as a natural learning place, and record keeping, and features sample forms and an extensive list of resources for providers.

Trawick-Smith, J., & L. Lambert. 1995. The unique challenges of the family child care provider: Implications for professional development. *Young Children* 50 (3): 25–32.

West, K. 1979. *Family day-to-day care*. Mound, MN: Quality Child Care. Series of articles, amusingly illustrated, on various aspects of family child care.

Program implementation

Aronson, S. 1983. Health update: Infection and day care. *Child Care Information Exchange* (March/April): 10–14.

Aronson, S. 1983. Health update: Health policies and procedure. *Child Care Information Exchange* (September/October): 14–16.

Badger, E. 1981. *Infant/toddler: Introducing your child to the joy of learning*. St. Paul, MN: Toys 'n Things Press, Resources for Child Caring. A sequence of learning activities that stress experiences in sensorimotor development matched to developmental levels; tells how to observe and record progress.

Brown, J. 1982. *Curriculum planning for young children*. Washington, DC: NAEYC.

Burtt, K.F., & K. Kalkstein. 1981. *Smart toys for babies from birth to two*. New York: Harper & Row. Describes 77 toys a baby will enjoy and learn from; includes clear line drawings and step-by-step instructions for constructing toys.

Dodge, DT. & L.J. Colker. 1991. *The creative curriculum for family child care*. Washington, DC: Teaching Strategies. Presents concrete strategies and approaches for providing developmentally appropriate care in the home.

Cataldo, C. 1983. Infant-toddler education: Blending the best approaches. *Young Children* 39 (2): 25–32.

Greenfield, P., & E. Tronick. 1980. *Infant curriculum: The Bromley-Heath guide to the care of infants in groups*. Santa Monica, CA: Goodyear. A practical guide to group care, including discussions of goals, values, and discipline techniques, suggestions for daily scheduling, and overview of infant development.

Highberger, R., & M. Boynton. 1983. Preventing illness in infant/toddler day care. *Young Children* 38 (3): 3–10.

Honig, A.S. 1979. What you need to know to select and train your day care staff. *Child Care Quarterly* 8 (1): 19–35.

Honig, A.S. 1982. Adding infants and toddlers to your program: Ten training tips. *Child Care Information Exchange* (May/June): 1–4.

Kendrick, A., R. Kaufmann, & K. Messenger, eds. 1995. *Healthy young children: A manual for programs.* Washington, DC: NAEYC.

National Academy of Early Childhood Programs. 1985. *Early childhood program description.* Washington, DC: NAEYC.

National Academy of Early Childhood Programs. 1985. *Guide to accreditation.* Washington, DC: NAEYC.

Sparling, J., & I. Lewis. 1979. *Learningames for the first three years: A guide to parent/child play.* New York: Walker. Describes 100 games that reflect typical patterns of infant development; provides checklists that can monitor the child's progress.

Partnership with parents

Bromwich, R. 1981. *Working with parents and infants: An interactional approach.* Baltimore, MD: University Park Press. Advocates the use of a problem-solving process to provide the kind of support, information, and encouragement that enables parents to discover solutions for themselves and their infants.

Galinsky, E. 1982. Understanding ourselves and parents. In *Caring for infants and toddlers: What works, what doesn't,* Vol. 2, eds. R. Lurie & R. Neugebauer, 65–70. Redmond, WA: Child Care Information Exchange.

Stone, J. 1987. *Teacher-parent relationships.* Washington, DC: NAEYC.

Honig, A.S. 1979. *Parent involvement in early childhood education,* rev. ed. Washington, DC: NAEYC.

Lurie, R., & K. Newman. 1982. A healthy tension: Parents and group infant/toddler care. In *Caring for infants and toddlers: What works, what doesn't,* Vol. 2, eds. R. Lurie & R. Neugebauer, 71–76. Redmond, WA: Child Care Information Exchange.

O'Connell, J.C. 1983. Research in review. Children of working mothers: What the research tells us. *Young Children* 38 (2): 62–70.

Powell, D.R. 1989. *Families and early childhood programs, Research Monographs Vol. 3.* Washington, DC: NAEYC.

Other resources

Brazelton, T.B. 1985. *Working and caring.* Menlo Park, CA: Addison-Wesley. Offers help on how to hold down a job and raise a child at the same time.

Brazelton, T.B. 1987. *What every baby knows.* Menlo Park, CA: Addison-Wesley. Based on a TV series, this book translates the film into words, offering parents a unique opportunity to experience the actual problems of real families.

Bredekamp, S., ed. 1987. *Developmentally appropriate practice in early childhood programs serving children from birth through age 8.* Washington, DC: NAEYC.

Carnegie Corporation of New York. *Starting points: Meeting the needs of our youngest children.* New York: Carnegie Task Force on Meeting the Needs of Young Children. This report of a blue-ribbon task force documents the "quiet crisis" affecting millions of children under 3 and their families and calls for integrated action in promoting responsible parenthood, guaranteeing quality child care choices and mobilizing communities to support young children and their families.

Dittman, L.L. 1993. *Finding the best care for your infant or toddler.* Washington, DC: NAEYC and Zero to Three/National Center for Clinical Infant Programs. Helps parents make informed choices about the options for caring for infants and toddlers.

Honig, A.S., & D.S. Wittmer. 1981. *Infant/toddler caregiving: An annotated bibliography.* Urbana, IL: ERIC, ED 215 781. Annotates books and audiovisual materials for continued reading in the area of infant/toddler development and caregiving.

Kagan, J., R. Kearsley, & P. Zelazo. 1980. *Infancy.* Cambridge, MA: Harvard University Press. A technical resource that discusses early experience and infant development research findings as well as the results of a study of a university-based infant child care program.

Diaper Changing Procedure

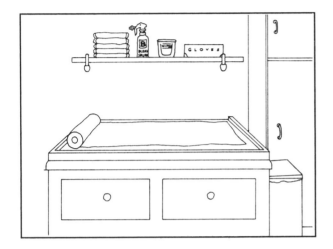

1. Get organized

- Before you bring the child to the diaper changing area, gather what you need: nonabsorbent paper, a fresh diaper, wipes, gloves if you use them, a plastic bag for any soiled clothes, and a dab of any diaper cream if the baby uses it. Take the supplies you will need out of the containers and put the containers away.

- Put on the disposable gloves, if you use them.

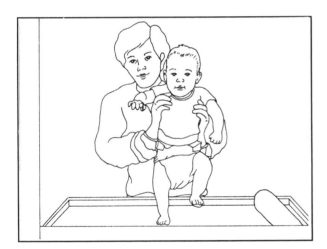

2. Avoid contact with soiled items, and always keep a hand on the baby

Anything that comes in contact with stool or urine is a source of germs.

- Carry the baby to the changing table, keeping soiled clothing away from you.

- Bag soiled clothes and securely tie the plastic bag to send them home.

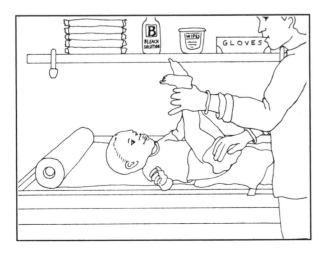

3. Clean the child's diaper area

- Unfasten the diaper, but leave the soiled diaper under the child.

- Use disposable wipes to clean the diaper area. Remove stool and urine from front to back and use a fresh wipe each time. Put the wipes into the soiled diaper.

- Note and report any skin problems such as redness.

4. Remove the soiled diaper and clean soiled surfaces

- Fold the diaper over and secure it with the tabs.
- Put it into a covered, lined step can.
- Check for spills under the baby.
- Remove the gloves and put them directly into the step can.
- Wipe your hands with a disposable wipe.

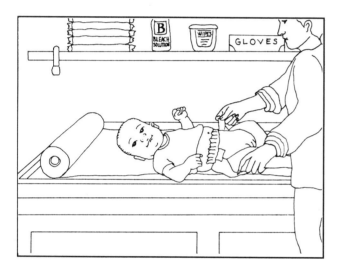

5. Put on a clean diaper

Slide the diaper under the baby, adjust and fasten it.

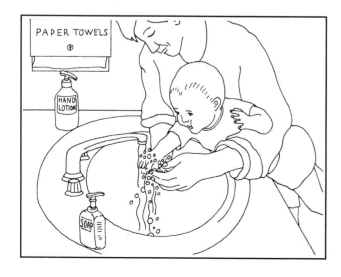

6. Clean the baby's hands

Use soap and water at a sink if you can. If a baby is too heavy to hold for handwashing at the sink, use disposable wipes or follow this procedure:

- Wipe the child's hands with a damp paper towel moistened with a drop of liquid soap.
- Wipe the child's hands with a paper towel wet with clear water.
- Dry the child's hands with a paper towel.

7. Clean and disinfect the diapering area

- Dispose of the table liner.
- Clean any visible soil from the changing table.
- Disinfect the table by spraying it so you wet the entire surface with bleach solution (1 tablespoon household bleach to 1 quart of water—mixed fresh daily).
- Leave the bleach on the surface for 2 minutes. The surface can then be wiped dry or left to air dry.

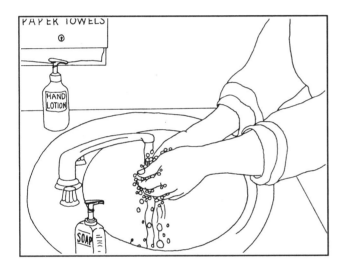

8. Wash your hands and record in the child's daily log

- Use soap and running warm water.
- Use a paper towel to turn off faucet.
- Use hand lotion to keep your hands from becoming dry and chapped.
- Record in daily log what was in the diaper and any problems.

Source: Adapted from *Healthy Young Children: A Manual for Programs*, 1988, eds. A.S. Kendrick, R. Kaufmann, & K.P. Messenger, 39–41. Washington, DC: NAEYC.

Handwashing procedures

- Wash hands upon arrival; before preparing food, eating, or feeding; and after toileting (self or a child) or handling bodily secretions (e.g., diapering, wiping a nose, cleaning up vomit or drool, handling soiled clothing or other contaminated items).
- Check to make sure a paper towel is available.
- Turn on water to a comfortable temperature. (Hot water supplied to fixtures that are accessible to children should not exceed 120° F).
- Moisten hands with water and apply heavy lather of *liquid* soap.
- Pay particular attention to areas between fingers, around nail beds, under fingernails, and backs of hands.
- Rinse well under running water until free of soap and dirt. Hold hands so that water flows from wrist to fingertips.
- Dry hands with paper towel.
- Use paper towel to turn off faucet; then discard towel.

(Kendrick, Kaufmann, & Messenger 1988, 33)

First Aid at a Glance

Ailment	Signs & Symptoms	First Aid

Poison	Symptoms vary greatly.
	Aids to determine whether poison was swallowed:
	a. information from victim or observer
	b. presence of poison container
	c. condition of victim (sudden onset of pain or illness)
	d. burns around lips
	e. breath odor
	f. pupil contracted to pinpoint size
		All victims
		    Call emergency rescue squad & Poison Control Center.
		    Save label or container for I.D.
		    Save sample of vomitus material.
		Conscious victims
		    Dilute poison with milk or water.
		    Do not give oils or neutralize with counteragents.
		Unconscious victims
		    Maintain open airway (place victim on side).
		    Give mouth-to-mouth resuscitation or CPR if necessary.
		    Do not give fluids; do not induce vomiting.
		Convulsions
		    Do not restrain victim; loosen tight clothing.
		    Watch for airway obstruction.
		    Do not give fluids or induce vomiting.

Shock	• Skin pale (or bluish), cold to touch; possibly moist or clammy • Weakness • Rapid pulse (over 100) • Usually increase in rate of breathing; may be shallow or deep and regular	Keep victim lying down. Cover only enough to prevent loss of body heat. Obtain medical help as soon as possible.
Fractures and Dislocations	• Pain and tenderness • Possible difficulty in moving injured part • Obvious deformities—swelling and discoloration	Keep broken bone ends and adjacent joints from moving. Give care for shock. Call for medical help.

Burns	Skin is
	a. red—1st degree
	b. blistered—2d degree
	c. charred—3d degree
		Pain of 1st-degree and small 2d-degree burns can be relieved by excluding air. Ways to keep air off burns are
		    a. submerge in cold water (do not use ice!)
		    b. apply a cold pack
		    c. cover with a thick dressing (do not apply grease or ointment)
		
		For a 3d-degree burn, cover with dry, clean cloth and call for medical help. If burn is in victim's face area, watch for possible need for artificial respiration.

Heart Attack	• Acute pain in chest, upper abdomen, or down left arm and shoulder • Extreme shortness of breath • Absence of pulse and breathing in an unconscious person	Place victim in comfortable position, usually sitting up. If not breathing, give artificial respiration. If no pulse is present, administer CPR. Call for medical help and give prescribed medication, if any. Do not give liquids to unconscious victims.
Loss of Consciousness	• Unresponsive	Keep victim warm and lying down, head turned to one side. If consciousness is not regained quickly, send for medical help. If breathing stops, give artificial respiration. Never give an unconscious person food or liquids.

Source: Adapted from information from the American Red Cross. Contact your local Red Cross chapter for more information about first aid procedures and about CPR training.

Developmental Sequence of Feeding Skills

Age (months)	Oral and neuro-muscular development	Feeding skills implications	Special notes
Birth to 1	Rooting reflex	Turns mouth toward nipple or object that brushes cheek	Breast-fed babies need vitamin D and fluoride supplements. Formula-fed babies need no supplements except possibly fluoride.
2 to 4	Sucking reflex	Begins when lips are touched	
	Swallowing reflex	Initially involves only the back of the tongue. By 9 to 12 weeks, the front will begin to become involved.	
4 to 6	Extrusion reflex		Pushes out any food placed on front of tongue
	Sucking reflex becomes voluntary		
	Holds head erect		
	Mouth poises for nipple—anticipates food/bottle on sight		
	Extrusion reflex diminishes, giving way to chewing motion	Begin introduction of solid foods as infant's need for calories and certain nutrients increases that cannot be provided by breast milk or formula alone	Start with rice cereal. Prepare with 1 tablespoon formula or breast milk. Gradually increase consistency as baby gets used to it.
	Begins to reach mouth with hand		
	Grasps objects voluntarily		
		Uses tongue to move food in mouth Texture of food may be increased	
	Moves jaw and tongue laterally Sits with support		
6 to 8	Puts lips to rim of cup	Begin to offer beverages from a cup	Breast milk or formula is still the most important food in baby's diet
	Puts most objects into mouth	Encourage finger food	
	Grasps spoon, nipple, or cup rim	Holds own bottle well. Removes food quickly from spoon with lips.	

Age (months)	Oral and neuro-muscular development	Feeding skills implications	Special notes
6 to 8 (cont.)	Sits without support for brief periods Begins voluntary biting and early chewing	Increase texture to soft, mashed table foods	Offer strained, mashed, or bite-size pieces of cooked or soft, fresh or canned fruits and vegetables
8 to 10	Sits without support	Feeds self finger foods. Use soft table foods cut in small pieces.	Wheat products may be started. Begin meat and poultry (chopped or strained) and eggs.*
10 to 12	Chews up and down Closes lips around rim of cup Has neat pincer grasp Ceases drooling Tries to use spoon Increased rotary motion of jaw	Gradually increase texture; offer whole fruits and vegetables Drinks from cup or glass with help Offer finger foods in small pieces	May try small amounts of whole-grain cereals
12 to 18	Growth rate slows considerably Increases independence	Tries to use spoon. Give some thick foods that will stick to spoon. Can chew meats Decreased appetite, may refuse food. Provide small amounts. Uses spoon, may be upside down. Mostly feeds self Holds glass/cup with two hands to drink Discards bottle	Cheese or yogurt may replace some milk

*Note: Because egg whites may promote allergies, some experts recommend not introducing eggs before 11 months.

Source: *Guidelines for Feeding Infants and Young Children* by Nutrition Services of Vermont Department of Health, Burlington, VT, 1979; revised 1991, 1993. Adapted with permission.

Appendix C

Food for Baby's First Year

The foods that a baby can eat depend on the baby's developmental readiness and nutritional needs. This guide describes the skills that are usually present at various ages and the foods that the baby is ready to eat.

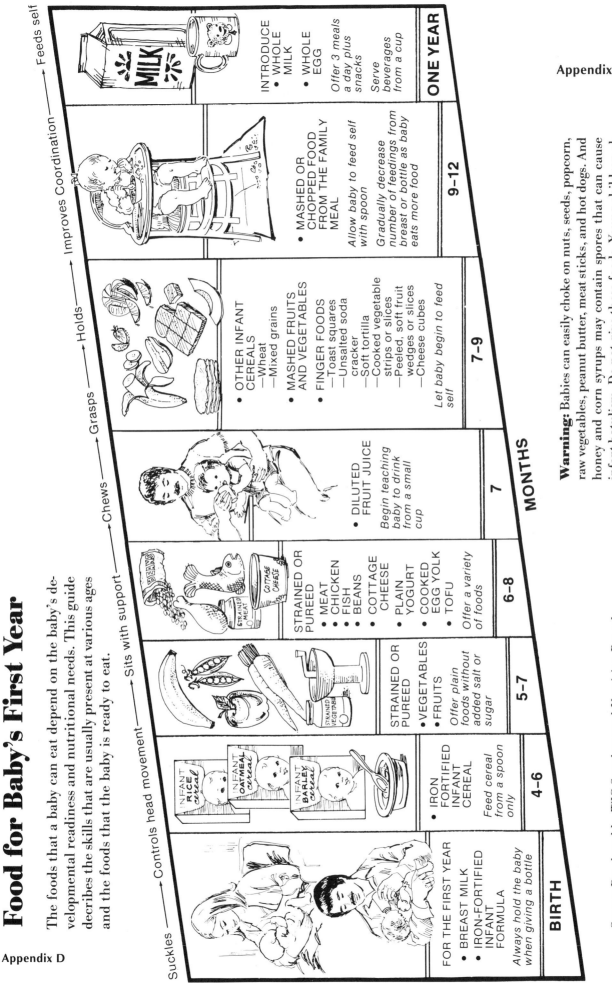

Suckles → Controls head movement → Sits with support → Chews → Grasps → Holds → Improves Coordination → Feeds self

BIRTH

FOR THE FIRST YEAR
• BREAST MILK
• IRON-FORTIFIED INFANT FORMULA

Always hold the baby when giving a bottle

4-6

• IRON FORTIFIED INFANT CEREAL

Feed cereal from a spoon only

5-7

STRAINED OR PUREED
• VEGETABLES
• FRUITS

Offer plain foods without added salt or sugar

6-8

STRAINED OR PUREED
• MEAT
• CHICKEN
• FISH
• BEANS
• COTTAGE CHEESE
• PLAIN YOGURT
• COOKED EGG YOLK
• TOFU

Offer a variety of foods

7

• DILUTED FRUIT JUICE

Begin teaching baby to drink from a small cup

7-9

• OTHER INFANT CEREALS
—Wheat
—Mixed grains
• MASHED FRUITS AND VEGETABLES
• FINGER FOODS
—Toast squares
—Unsalted soda cracker
—Soft tortilla
—Cooked vegetable strips or slices
—Peeled, soft fruit wedges or slices
—Cheese cubes

Let baby begin to feed self

9-12

• MASHED OR CHOPPED FOOD FROM THE FAMILY MEAL

Allow baby to feed self with spoon

Gradually decrease number of feedings from breast or bottle as baby eats more food

ONE YEAR

INTRODUCE
• WHOLE MILK
• WHOLE EGG

Offer 3 meals a day plus snacks

Serve beverages from a cup

MONTHS

Warning: Babies can easily choke on nuts, seeds, popcorn, raw vegetables, peanut butter, meat sticks, and hot dogs. And honey and corn syrups may contain spores that can cause infant botulism. Do not give these foods. Young children always should be closely watched when they are eating.

Source: Developed by WIC Supplemental Nutrition Branch, California Department of Health Services.

Common Toddler Phrases in

English	Spanish	French
good morning	buenos días	bonjour
bye-bye	adiós	au revoir
Where is Mommy?	¿Dónde está mami?	Oú est Maman?
There is Mommy.	Allí está mami.	Voilà Maman!
Mommy will be back.	Mami va a regresar.	Maman va revenir.
juice	jugo	jus
singing	cantando	chantant
no	no	non
not safe	peligroso	dangereux
I am going to help you.	Yo te voy a ayudar.	Je vais t'aider.
Stop!	¡Parar!	Arretez!
It is okay.	Está bien.	C'est d'accord.
great	muy bien	formidable
sad, angry	triste, enojado	triste, fâché
finished	terminado	fini
Wait!	¡Espera!	Attendez!
want	quiero	veux
daddy, brother, sister, child, children	papi (or padre), hermano, hermana, niño, niños	papa, frère, soeur, enfant, enfants
soon	pronto	bientôt
I don't understand.	No entiendo.	Je ne comprends pas.
Show me.	Muestrame.	Montrez-moi.
slower, faster	más despacio, más fuerte	plus doucement, plus vite
a little	un poco	un peu
Let's go.	¡Vamos!	Allons-y!
baby	bebé	bebe
Can you tell me in English?	¿Puedes me lo decir en inglés?	Peux-tu me dire en Anglias?
give	¡Démelo!	donne
big, little	grande, pequeña (fem.), pequeño (masc.)	grand, petite (fem.), petit (mas.)
up, down	arriba, abajo	en l'air, en bas
high, low	alto, bajo	haut, bas
toys, games	juegos, juguetes	jouet/joujou, crâne
where	dónde	ou
I, you	yo, tú	je, tu
snack time	hora de comer la merienda	gouter
good-bye song	canción de adiós	chanson
time to put away toys	tiempo de guardar los juguetes	c'est le moment de ranger les jouets

5 Languages

Hebrew	*Farsi*
boker tov	sob bekair
shalom	khodafes/khodahafez
Eifoh Immah?	Maman kojas(t)/koo?
Hineh Immah.	Maman anjas(t).
Imma tachzor.	Maman halla miyad.
mitz	abe meeve
lashir	avaz mikhanad
lo	na
zeh mesukan	khatarnak
Ani eezov lecha (lach).	Man be to komak mikonam.
Atzor!	Vaist!
Zeh besseder.	Doroste, khoobe.
yoffi	kheylee khoob, alee
atzuv, koess	narahat, asabani
nigmar	tamam shod
Chakeh!	Sabr kon!
rotzeh	khastan
abba, ach, achot, yeled, yeladim	baba, baradar, khahar, bache, bacheha
odd meaat	zood
Ani lo mevina.	Man nemifahmam.
Tireh li.	Neshanam bede.
yoter leaat, yoter maher	yavashtar, tondtar
ketzat	ye kami
Boh, nelech	Berim.
tinok	bache
Tagid li Beaanglit?	Mitooni be ingilisi begi?
ten li	bede be man
gadol, kattan	bozorg, koochek
lemala, lematta	baala, paeen
gavoha, namooch	baala, paeen
tzaatzua	asbaabe bazi
eifoh	koja/koo
Ani, atta	man, tow
ochel	moghe ghaza
lashir bye bye	ahange khodahafesi
zman lesader et hatzaatzuim	vaghte kenar guzashtane asbabe bazi

Source: Adapted from *Parent/Toddler Group,* P. Rothman & I. van der Zande, Los Angeles, Cedars-Sinai Medical Center Foundation, 1990. With additional help in translation/transliteration from Halina Cymerman, Washington, DC; Anika Trahan, NAEYC; Zelman Alpert, Yeshiva University; and Faroog Hamid, University of Pennsylvania.

Infant Care Center Permission to Give Medication

The LCPC Infant Care Center shall administer medications for children only when requested by the prescribing physician. Each container shall be childproof and carry the name of the medication, the name of the person for whom it was prescribed, the name of the prescribing physician, and the physician's instructions. Each child's medication shall be stored in its original container. No medication shall be transferred between containers. This is in compliance with state and federal laws.

Child's Name _____

Prescription Name and Number _____

Pharmacy Name _____

Physician's Name _____ Phone # _____

Description of Medication (i.e., yellow capsules, pink liquid) _____
_____

Condition Requiring Medication _____

Amount To Be Taken _____ Time of Day To Be Given _____

Precautions _____ DP _____

Date To Be Discontinued _____

_____   _____
Signature of Parent   Date

Medication Given

	Date	Time	By		Date	Time	By
1.				10.			
2.				11.			
3.				12.			
4.				13.			
5.				14.			
6.				15.			
7.				16.			
8.				17.			
9.				18.			

Source: La Canada Presbyterian Church, La Canada, California

Samples of Daily Report Forms

DAILY PARENT INFORMATION

Child's Name _____ Date _____ Arrival Time _____

1. Last evening my child had the following foods:

   _____

   _____

   _____

2. A. How long did she/he sleep last night? _____

   B. What time did she/he get up this morning? _____

   C. Did she/he sleep well? If the answer to 2C is "no," what seemed to be the problem
      (i.e., diarrhea, fever, etc.)? _____

   _____

3. Did she/he have a bowel movement this morning? _____

4. Did your baby have breakfast this morning? _____

   If yes, what time and what did she/he eat? _____

   _____

5. What liquids or solids did you bring today? _____

   _____

6. Is there any other information that will help us take better care of your baby? _____

   _____

   _____

   _____

   Parent

Source: Centinela Hospital Child Care Center, Inglewood, California

PARENT/STAFF DAILY CONTACT SHEET

white Copy—Center file
yellow Copy—Parent

Child's Name _____

Date: _____ Time In: _____ Time Out: _____

What time did your child awake? _____ Mood: _____

Has he had breakfast? _____ Time: _____

Milk? _____ Other foods? _____

Any special needs? _____

Other comments by Parent: _____

CARE GIVEN OR OBSERVATION

	Time	Initials
Ate (food, quantity, times, initials)		
Slept (when, how long)		
Diaper changes (bowel movements, time, record rashes, etc.)		
Other information (medications, new activities, etc.)		

To Parents: _____

_____

Conference with Parent By: _____

Parent Signature: _____

Source: Kids Will Be Kids, Inc., Ontario, California

DAILY INFORMATION FOR PARENTS FROM CAREGIVERS

Child's Name _____ Date _____

What she/he ate today:

Breakfast _____ Time _____

Snack _____ AM _____ PM _____

Lunch _____ Time _____

Dinner _____ Time _____

Bottles: Time _____ Amt. _____ Time _____ Amt. _____ Time _____ Amt. _____

Naps: AM _____ _____ PM _____ _____

Bowel Movement: _____ _____ _____ _____

Total Diapers Used: _____

Special Happenings: _____

Needs: _____

Comments: _____

DAILY INFORMATION FOR CAREGIVERS
FROM THE PARENT

1. When, what, and how much did your baby eat or drink last?

   a. Time _____

   b. Type of food _____

   c. Amount _____

2. How long did she/he sleep last night? _____

   What time did she/he get up this morning? _____

   Did she/he sleep well? _____

   If she/he did not sleep well, what seemed to be the problem?

_____

_____

   Did she/he have a bowel movement today? _____

3. Is there any other information that will help us take better care of your baby today?

_____

_____

Source: La Canada Presbyterian Church Infant Care Center, La Canada, California

INFANT/TODDLER INFORMATION SHEET

Child's Name _____

Week of _____

	MONDAY	TUESDAY	WEDNESDAY	THURSDAY	FRIDAY
FEEDINGS					
SOLID FOOD					
BMs					
URINATION					
SLEPT					

Comments: _____

_____

_____

_____

Source: St. Luke's Child Care Center, Pasadena, California.

PARENT REPORT FORM

Child's Name _____

Child's Health _____

Time of Last Feeding _____

Medication _____

Special Instructions _____

_____

_____

CARE GIVEN BY STAFF

Food or Bottles   Quantity   Time

_____

_____

_____

_____

_____

SLEEPING

Time Asleep   Time Awake

_____

_____

_____

_____

Other Information:

Source: Lanterman State Hospital, California

Appendix G   123

INFANT/TODDLER PROGRAM

Childs' Name _____ Date _____

Parents: Please indicate in "Home" column your child's schedule today before he came to school. Indicate what he ate, diaper changes (whether wet, dry, or bowel movement), napping, etc. Show approximate time. Also in "Home" column please indicate approximate schedule of meals, food and amount, and sleeping schedule you would like our staff to follow for your child.

Staff: In "School" column, please indicate time, item (nap, diaper change, or meal) and initial. Be specific about foods, diaper (wet, dry, or bowel movement), and napping.

HOME Time	Item	SCHOOL Time	Item	Initial

Infant's Name _____ Time of Arrival _____ Date _____

Naptime _____

Feeding Times

Diaper Changes

Other Information

Person Reporting _____

Source: Church of the Good Shepherd Nursery School, Arcadia, California

DAILY STAFF REPORT

Child's Name _____ Date _____ Staff _____

_____

FEEDING

FOOD	AMOUNT	TIME	COMMENTS	INIT.

DIAPER CHANGE

VOIDED	STOOL	TIME	COMMENTS	INIT.

SLEEP

TIME	COMMENTS	INIT.

MEDICATION

PRESCRIPTION INFORMATION	TIME	INIT.

COMMENTS

STAFF	PARENT

Source: Centinela Hospital Child Care Center, Inglewood, California

DAILY LOG

Child's Name:

	MON.	TUES.	WEDS.	THURS.	FRI.
ATE					
LIQUIDS					
SLEPT					
BMs					
MESSAGES TO PARENTS					
MESSAGES TO STAFF					

Source: Parent Infant Care Services, Inc., Ocean Park, California

Information About NAEYC

NAEYC is . . .

a membership-supported organization of people committed to fostering the growth and development of children from birth through age 8. Membership is open to all who share a desire to serve and act on behalf of the needs and rights of young children.

NAEYC provides . . .

educational services and resources to adults who work with and for children, including

- *Young Children*, *the* journal for early childhood educators
- **books, posters, brochures,** and **videos** to expand your knowledge and commitment to young children, with topics including infants, curriculum, research, discipline, teacher education, and parent involvement
- an **Annual Conference** that brings people together from all over the country to share their expertise and advocate on behalf of children and families
- **Week of the Young Child** celebrations sponsored by NAEYC Affiliate Groups across the nation to call public attention to the needs and rights of children and families
- **insurance plans** for individuals and programs
- **public affairs** information and access to information available through NAEYC resources and communication systems for knowledgeable advocacy efforts at all levels of government and through the media
- the **National Academy of Early Childhood Programs,** a voluntary accreditation system for high-quality programs for children
- the **National Institute for Early Childhood Professional Development,** which offers resources and services to improve professional preparation and development of early childhood educators
- **Young Children International** to promote international communication and information exchanges

For free information about membership, publications, or other NAEYC services, contact

**National Association for the Education
of Young Children**
1509 16th Street, NW
Washington, DC 20036-1426
202-232-8777 or 1-800-424-2460